Bloom's Morning

BLOOM'S

MORNING

Coffee, Comforters, and the Secret Meaning of Everyday Life

Arthur Asa Berger

WestviewPress

A Division of HarperCollins*Publishers*

Published in 1997 in the United States of America by Westview Press, 5500 Central Avenue, Boulder, Colorado, 80301-2877, and in the United Kingdom by Westview Press, 12 Hid's Copse Road, Cumnor Hill, Oxford OX2 9JJ

Library of Congress Cataloging-in-Publication Data
Berger, Arthur Asa, 1933–
    Bloom's morning : coffee, comforters, and the secret meaning of everyday life / Arthur Asa Berger.
        p.   cm.
    Includes bibliographical references (p.   ) and index.
    ISBN 0-8133-3230-3
    1. Morning customs—United States.   2. Social psychology—United States.   3. United States—Social life and customs—20th century.
4. Postmodernism—Social aspects.   5. Semiotics.   I. Title.
GT3002.3.U6B47   1997
392—dc20   96-24717
                                                                    CIP

Design by Jane Raese. Illustrations by Arthur Asa Berger.

The paper used in this publication meets the requirements of the American National Standard for Permanence of Paper for Printed Library Materials Z39-1984.

10   9   8   7   6   5   4   3   2   1

Contents

PART ONE
Introduction

PART TWO
Ulysses Sociologica

Contents

PART THREE
Conclusion

Preface

This study of everyday life in American culture was inspired by two books—James Joyce's *Ulysses* and Sigmund Freud's *The Interpretation of Dreams*. From Joyce I got the idea of taking as my subject (or central conceit) twenty-four hours in the life of a person, and from Freud I got the device of writing a short narrative and then dealing with the significance of its every word or phrase.

My book, unlike Joyce's, is not fiction—though some would dispute that assertion. It is, broadly speaking, "sociological," or perhaps "sociosemiotic" . . . whatever that means. It attempts to interpret the social, psychological, and cultural significance of the various objects one encounters in a typical day. Actually, because there is so much material, I deal not with an entire day . . . but instead with only the morning of our hero. I have called him, in deference to Joyce, Leopold Bloom . . . but he could easily have been called Bill Smith or any other name. Hence the title of this book, *Bloom's Morning*.

In the second chapter of Freud's *The Interpretation of Dreams* there is a wonderful analysis by Freud of one of his own dreams. He took a page to write down the events he remembered from his dream and a number of pages to analyze the most important phrases or sentences in his narrative. I have adopted this format: I offer a short narrative describing Bloom's morning, and this is followed by more than thirty essays, each of which analyzes the significance of an activity or artifact mentioned by Bloom from the moment he is wakened by his clock radio until he gets his morning mail.

My methodology of analysis is, you will soon discover, heavily influenced by semiotics, Freudian psychoanalytic theory, and the work of Mircea Eliade, so do not be surprised if you encounter a good deal of sex and religion (both generally in camouflaged forms) in these essays.

If one were to go to some preliterate tribe in the middle of Africa or the Amazon or some far-off land and make the kind of analysis found in this book, nobody would think twice about it. That is what many anthropologists do, and it is considered okay as long as it is done to others. And the more we find out about the foods other cultures eat, the objects they use, their myths, their folklore, their rites, and their sexual practices, the better the research is held to be and the happier people (in general) are about it.

I have taken the standard anthropological fascination with material culture (and the social and economic fabric in which it is embedded) and subjected it to analysis. Why not? America is a fabulous country where all kinds of bizarre things go on. Why go abroad when this society is so incredible? Or at least (and this is particularly important because we're running out of preliterate tribes and travel money), why not turn more attention to American culture?

I don't know why this country isn't crawling with anthropologists studying our remarkable subcultures, cults, fads, fashions, food habits, rites, rituals, sexual practices, myths, games, and fanaticisms of one sort or another. Because we live here we don't recognize it, but this is a very strange country full of strange people.

My essays are all quite brief. Each can be read within the eight-minute attention span that is the norm here in America (the amount of time between television commercials). I hope you will find the analyses instructive and entertaining, and that as a result of reading this book you will see some old and familiar things in new ways.

I have illustrated each of the chapters with my own spot drawings and hope they will add a pleasing visual element to the book.

Arthur Asa Berger

Acknowledgments

I would like thank my editor, Gordon Massman, for his encouragement and his wonderful assistance with this book. I would also like to thank his assistant, Jennifer Chen, and the staff at Westview Press for everything they've done to bring this book into being.

I have also benefited from the work of many writers who provided me with insights and made me believe that a book on material culture and everyday life in the United States might be of interest to many. Among these writers are Roland Barthes, Umberto Eco, Sigmund Freud, James Joyce, and Georges Perec.

A.A.B.

PART 1

Introduction

There is a series of phenomena of great importance which cannot possibly be recorded by questioning or computing documents, but have to be observed in their full actuality. Let us call them the imponderabilia of actual life. Here belong such things as the routine of a man's working day, the details of his care of the body, of the manner of taking food and preparing it; the tone of conversational and social life around the village fires, the existence of strong friendships or hostilities, and of passing sympathies and dislikes between people; the subtle yet unmistakable manner in which personal vanities and ambitions are reflected in the behaviour of the individual and in the emotional reactions of those who surround him. All these facts can and ought to be scientifically formulated and recorded, but it is necessary that this be done, not by a superficial registration of details, as is usually done by untrained observers, but with an effort at penetrating the mental attitude expressed in them.

—Bronislaw Malinowski,
Argonauts of the Western Pacific

On the Theory of Everyday Life

(Ulysses Sociologica, or Bloom's Morning)

In recent decades the study of culture has assumed a centrality it never had before. This is because we now recognize that in its numerous dimensions from mass-mediated popular culture to elite works of art, culture has consequences and is not a mere epiphenomenon tied to social, economic, and political arrangements found in societies.

On the Development of Cultural Studies

We used to distinguish between elite culture and popular culture, and we dismissed popular culture as subliterary and trivial. There was also a split between the anthropological view of culture, which dealt with all the activities people engage in and that are passed on from generation to generation, and an aesthetic perspective, which focused on works of art, primarily what were seen as elite arts (poetry, classical music, theater, novels, and that kind of thing).

The anthropological perspective defines culture as "that complex whole which includes knowledge, belief, art, morals, law, custom, and any other capabilities and habits acquired by man as a member of society" (Davis and Schleifer 1991, 8). As Robert Con Davis and Ronald Schleifer write in *Criticism and Culture*, according to Claude Lévi-Strauss, the influential French anthropologist, "The distinguishing feature of culture as opposed to nature is that culture is everywhere *meaningful*, everywhere imbued with signification, meaning itself is the *effect* of logical, intellectual structures by which the mind orders experience" (1991, 8). We have conflated all of these definitions of culture, and a relatively new field of studies has emerged: cultural studies, which deals with all aspects of culture, from simple objects used in our everyday lives to serious novels and plays and everything in between, including comic books, television programs, formulaic fiction, and sports, among other things.

The development of postmodernist thought has played an important part in the evolution of cultural studies. As Mike Featherstone reminds us in *Consumer Culture and Postmodernism:* "Amongst the central features associated with postmodernism in the arts are: the effacement of the boundary between art and everyday life; the collapse of the hierarchical distinction between high and mass/popular culture; a stylistic promiscuity favouring eclecticism and the mixing of codes; parody, pastiche, irony, playfulness and the celebration of the surface 'depthlessness' of culture; the decline of the originality/genius of the artistic producer; and the assumption that art can only be repetitive" (1991, 7–8). As a result of the development of postmodernist thought, we now have a much more comprehensive definition of culture, which leads to different ideas about how to analyze it and make sense of it. We no longer believe that we must focus all of our attention on "the best that has been thought and said" (as Matthew Arnold put it), and we have widened our range considerably to include what might be described as "the worst that has been thought and said" and everything in between. This new sensibility is, in part, tied to the acceptance of the anthropological view of culture by contemporary culture critics, who blend it with their traditional interests in what we used to call the elite arts.

Culture is no longer decontextualized, no longer thought of as just "frosting on the cake of life" or as something relatively obscure and irrelevant, an academic pursuit to occupy literature professors, communications scholars, effete arty types, and dilettantes. This older view saw culture as perhaps interesting and possibly enjoyable but not as part of everyday life or of any real significance. Culture, as those involved in cultural studies now tend to think of it, permeates every aspect of life and thus plays a central role in explaining how our societies and economies function and, in turn, how individuals are shaped.

The Importance of Everyday Life

I first became interested in everyday life when I read Johan Huizinga's *The Waning of the Middle Ages*, originally published in 1924. In this book, a study of art, thought, and life in France and the Netherlands in the fourteenth and fifteenth centuries, Huizinga writes: "The Middle Ages never forgot that all things would be absurd, if their meaning were exhausted in their function and their place in the phenomenal world, if by their essence they did not reach into a world beyond this. This idea of a deeper significance in ordinary things is familiar to us as well, independently of religious convictions: as an indefinite feeling which may be called up at any moment, by the sound of raindrops on the leaves or by the lamplight on a table" (1924, 201). A few paragraphs after this, Huizinga quotes William James, who writes in *The Varieties of Religious Experience* that "when we see all things in God, and refer all things to Him, we read in common matters superior expressions of meaning" (1924, 202). This, Huizinga explains, is the psychological foundation of symbolism. "In God," he adds, "nothing is empty of sense . . . so the conviction of a transcendental meaning in all things seeks to formulate itself" (1924, 202).

Commonplace matters, routine events, and ordinary objects have, Huizinga suggests, symbolic meaning. And it is the duty of the cultural critic, and in particular the analyst of everyday life, to consider objects, activities, and routines that seem at first sight commonplace and insignificant as having meanings, transcendental and otherwise. That is, these phenomena can be looked upon as signs that lend themselves to analysis and interpretation. Their meaning is not exhausted in their function, though most people are blind to the meaning of objects because they are so involved with their functions and, in some cases, with the sense of power that comes from having and using them.

The Mechanical Bride

In 1951 Marshall McLuhan published *The Mechanical Bride*, a classic study of everyday life. In the preface to the book he makes a number of important methodological points. First, he tells us that the "exhibits" he deals with "have been selected because of their typical and familiar quality" (1967, v). That is, they are part of everyday life. Second, they reflect a number of social myths or forms and "speak a language we both know and do not know" and are part of our contemporary folklore. He writes, "But amid the diversity of our inventions and abstract techniques of production and distribution there will be found a great degree of cohesion and unity. This consistency is not conscious in origin or effect and seems to arise from a sort of collective dream. For that reason, as well as because of the widespread popularity of these objects and processes, they are here referred to as 'the folklore of industrial man'" (1967, v). The "exhibits" (as he calls them) are "not selected to prove a case but to reveal a complex situation." He cautions his readers that he is attempting to release some of the meaning of his topics and does not claim to exhaust their meaning.

The ideas and concepts McLuhan uses, he explains, are part of what might be called "probes" and are meant to be taken as points of departure in analyzing his various topics, not as conclusions he reaches about them. As he puts it, "Concepts are provisional affairs for apprehending reality; their value is in the grip they provide. This book, therefore, tries to present at once representative aspects of the reality and a wide range of ideas for taking hold of it" (1967, v). In essence, what he is doing, he tells us, is to apply methods traditionally used in the analysis of arts (by which he means elite arts) to "the critical evaluation of society." What this use of art criticism does is enable him to discover the means people use to obtain the effects they want and to consider whether obtaining these effects is worthwhile.

The Mechanical Bride is a large-format book (eight by ten inches) that contains fifty-nine discrete essays—on everything from the front page of the *New York Times* (his first essay) to a study of horse operas and popular culture (his last essay). He deals primarily with advertisements for various products (and with some comics), which he uses as a means of talking about the products they are selling and the values they reinforce. Each of his fifty-nine essays is illustrated in various ways, such as with an advertisement or a frame from a comic strip or the cover of a popular book or magazine.

McLuhan's goal is to probe the hidden beliefs and values reflected in the copy used in the advertisement and in the role the product plays in American society and culture. He also offers in most of his essays four or five questions and elliptical statements (in bold print) that deal with his topic. Let me offer an example or two.

He has an essay called "Know How" that shows an advertisement of a product called the Thor Automatic Gladiron. The ad is reproduced on the left half of the page. On the bottom of the right-hand side of the page we find the following:

How much more Know-How is needed to make human life obsolete? Is there any known gadget for controlling a rampant Know-How? The lady in the ad has found a mechanical substitute for moral choice? King Midas knew how to change everything into gold. Where did all that popcorn come from?

Above this material we find the first paragraph of his essay, which reads as follows:

As the ad implies, know-how is at once a technical and moral sphere. It is a duty for a woman to love her husband and also to love that soap that will make her husband love her. It is a duty to be glamorous, cheerful, efficient, and so far as is possible to run the home like an automatic factory. This ad also draws attention to the tendency of the modern housewife, after a premarital embrace in the business world, to embrace marriage and children, but not housework. . . . And so the ad promises her a means of doing physical work without hating the husband who has trapped her into household drudgery.

To purchase gadgets that relieve this drudgery and thus promote domestic affection is, therefore, a duty, too.

This leads McLuhan to discuss a number of related matters involving how "know-how" can be applied to love, success, and happiness; the ideas of Joseph Campbell's *The Hero with a Thousand Faces* and Werner Sombart's *Quintessence of Capitalism;* as well as the ideas of Lewis Mumford and Norbert Weiner as they relate to "know-how" and technology and the mechanization of everyday life.

The Puritans, McLuhan points out, retained the scholastic method in their theology, which they expressed in their austere secular existence. This method informs great modern businesses, which, McLuhan suggests, are connected to "some of the most striking features of medieval scholastic culture," except that they have transferred their zeal from theology to sales and distribution. That is why there is such a religious intensity found in the business world and in our attitudes toward modern technology.

He quotes a *Fortune* magazine article that suggests computers will someday be switched from directing guns to running factories and writes, "How persistently the face of murderous violence associates itself with know-how" (1967, 34). This leads him to discuss how executives think of producing and selling in "military terms, smashing public resistance with carefully planned barrages followed by shock troops of salesmen to mop up the pockets" (1967, 34).

Know-how, he reminds us, or the dream of technology that know-how represents, is hard to control and keep in a subordinate role: "Harnessed merely to a variety of blind appetites for power and success, it draws us swiftly into that labyrinth at the end of which waits the minotaur" (1967, 34).

If we can develop our rational self-awareness we can cultivate reasonable ways of restraining ourselves, but, he warns us at the conclusion of his essay, the process is difficult.

What McLuhan was doing in *The Mechanical Bride* was using advertisements (and the objects and products they are selling), comics, and other aspects of our popular culture to analyze everyday life in North America. He did this by recognizing that his advertisements and comics were signs that held a great deal of meaning. He did not use the language of semiotics per se, but his enterprise was semiotic in nature, and *The Mechanical Bride* is one of the classic modern studies of everyday life, even if it is not generally recognized as such.

From McLuhan we move to the work of Roland Barthes, a semiotician whose work is currently very much in vogue and whose work on everyday life is recognized for its intellectual audacity as well as its stylistic brilliance.

Roland Barthes's *Mythologies*

Roland Barthes was one of the most important contemporary cultural critics to alert us to the meanings and myths that can be found in common objects and everyday activities. He offers a remarkable analysis of contemporary everyday life in France in his celebrated book *Mythologies*. As he writes in the preface to the 1970 edition of his book, "I had just read Saussure and as a result acquired the conviction that by treating 'collective representations' as sign-systems, one might hope to go further than the pious show of unmasking them and account *in detail* for the mystification which transforms petit-bourgeois culture into a universal nature" (1972, 9).

His preface to the original edition of the book contains another description of his method. The essays in the book were, he tells us, written in each month between 1954 and 1956 and were informed by his notion that the naturalness of the topics he found interesting masked the historical and ideological aspects of things.

His focus, he adds, was on "what-goes-without-saying," on aspects of his topics that seemed ordinary and natural and that masked hidden ideological imperatives. What his topics have in common, he writes, is that they are repeated: "For while I don't know whether, as the saying goes, 'Things which are repeated are pleasing,' my belief is that they are significant. And what I sought throughout this book were significant features" (1972, 12).

Is this significance read into the objects he deals with? No doubt, he says, but he objects to the notion that there is a split between the so-called objectivity of the scientist and the subjectivity of what he calls the writer and what we would call the cultural analyst. It isn't that simple.

And what does Barthes, one of the most sophisticated and astute critics in France, deal with in *Mythologies*? A list of some of his topics is most revealing: televised wrestling (the first essay in the book), how filmmakers suggest "Roman-ness" in films, soap powders and detergents, margarine, *Elle* magazine, French toys, wine and milk, steak and *frites*, Einstein's brain, striptease, and the D.S.19 Citroen. His subjects are, then, part of people's lives—what they eat, what they use to clean their clothes, what they drive, and that kind of thing.

Let us consider a typical essay in *Mythologies*, the essay "Soap Powders and Detergents." He starts with a discussion of the First World Detergent Congress, held in Paris in September 1954, and with Omo (a French detergent) euphoria. He writes, "These products have been in the last few years the object of such massive advertising that they now belong to a region of French daily life which the various types of psycho-analysis would do well to pay attention to if they wish to keep up to date" (1972, 36). Barthes distinguishes between purifying (chlorinated) liquids, soap powders, and detergents. These chlorinated liquids, he suggests, are experienced as a kind of "liquid fire" that generate a "violent, abrasive modification of matter" and "kill dirt." Soap powders like Persil, however, are "separating agents" that liberate garments from dirt. They are also

11

selective and function, psychoanalytically speaking, to keep the public order. And the advertisements for Persil that stress "Persil whiteness" base their appeal on "the evidence of a result" (1972, 37). Detergents such as Omo work in different ways: They make the user an accomplice in the liberation of dirt rather than the mere beneficiary of the liberation.

Barthes shows how an advertisement for Omo about cleaning deeply and being foamy yields some interesting insights. He writes, "To say that *Omo* cleans in depth (see the Cinema-Publicite advertisement) is to assume that linen is deep, which no one had previously thought, and this unquestionably results in exalting it, by establishing it as an object favourable to those obscure tendencies to enfold and caress which are found in every human body. As for foam, it is well known that it signifies luxury" (1972, 37). The ad also suggests, Barthes adds, that matter is airy and foam is somehow spiritual in that it makes "something out of nothing." Ultimately, this foamy substance is used to disguise the abrasive quality of detergents. Where detergents and soap powders become "unified," he points out, is at the plane of ownership, for Unilever, the giant Dutch conglomerate, owns both Omo and Persil.

Thus, seemingly simple and banal products such as soap powders and detergents yield extremely interesting insights about values, beliefs, and attitudes people have—not only about soaps but also about linen (that it is deep), foam (that it has a spiritual nature), and a number of other things.

Empire of Signs

Let me turn now to another book of Barthes's, *Empire of Signs*, which is a fascinating and unique analysis of objects in a culture. Unlike *Mythologies*, which is based on Barthes's analysis of French culture, *Empire of Signs* deals with Japan—a culture foreign to Barthes. This book, written in 1970, uses his interest in commonplace objects and activities as a means of making sense of Japan, a "system," as he puts it, very different from the one found in France. He writes:

> The author has never, in any sense, photographed Japan. Rather, he has done the opposite: Japan has starred him with any number of "flashes"; or, better still, Japan has afforded him a situation of writing. This situation is the very one in which a certain disturbance of the person occurs, a subversion of earlier readings, a shock of meaning lacerated, extenuated to the point of its irreplaceable voice, without the objects ever ceasing to be significant, desirable. Writing is, after all, in its way, a *satori: satori* (the Zen occurrence) is a more or less powerful (though in no way formal) seism which causes knowledge, or the subject, to vacillate: it creates *an emptiness of language*. And it is also an emptiness of language which constitutes writing; it is from the emptiness that derive the features which Zen, in an exemption from all meaning, writes gardens, gestures, houses, flower arrangements, faces, and violence. (1982, 4)

What Barthes is arguing here is that he is attempting not to make a scholarly, systematic study of Japanese culture but to seize upon certain topics that strike his attention and to analyze them.

And what does Barthes write about in Japan? He has essays about Japanese food (in general), chopsticks, sukiyaki, tempura, *pachinko,* the design of Tokyo (a city with an "empty" center), train stations, packages, bowing, Haiku, Bunraku, eyelids, Japanese bodies, *Zengakuren* riots, and the organization of space, among other things. In each case he uses his subjects as "openings" that help him discover interesting things about Japanese culture. And it is because he knows so little about

Japanese culture, because it is so mysterious to him, that he is able to make his reading of Japanese culture so fresh and so penetrating.

Thus, his analysis of tempura in a chapter called "The Interstice" points out that tempura reverses things and strips fried food of the meaning we traditionally attach to it—heaviness. He adds:

> It is said that *tempura* is a dish of Christian (Portuguese) origin: it is the food of lent (*tempora*); but refined by the Japanese techniques of cancellation and exemption, it is the nutriment of another time: not of a rite of fasting and expiation, but of a kind of meditation, as much spectacular as alimentary (since *tempura* is prepared before your eyes), around an item we ourselves select, lacking anything better (and perhaps by reason of our thematic ruts), on the side of the light, the aerial, of the instantaneous, the fragile, the transparent, the crisp, the trifling, but whose real name would be *the interstice* without specific edges, or again: the empty sign. (1982, 25–26)

Tempura must be seen as something created by an artist, whose meaning is in its creation. It is we who eat the tempura, he writes of the chefs who cook it, "but it is he who has played, who has written, who has produced" (1982, 26).

Methodological Considerations: The Semiotic Challenge

Barthes deals with the subject of how to analyze objects such as tempura or soap powders in considerable detail in his essay

"The Kitchen of Meaning" (in his book *The Semiotic Challenge,* translated by Richard Howard). He writes,

> A garment, an automobile, a dish of cooked food, a gesture, a film, a piece of music, an advertising image, a piece of furniture, a newspaper headline—these indeed appear to be heterogeneous objects.
> What might they have in common? This at least: all are signs. When I walk through the streets—or through life—and encounter all these objects, I apply to all of them, if need be without realizing it, one and the same activity, which is that of a certain *reading:* modern man, urban man, spends his time reading. He reads, first of all and above all, images, gestures, behaviors: this car tells me the social status of its owner, this garment tells me quite precisely the degree of its wearer's conformism or eccentricity, this *apéritif* (whiskey, pernod, or white wine and cassis) reveals my host's life style. (1988, 147)

This search for meaning in seemingly trivial and ordinary objects is also at the heart of *Empire of Signs.*

These objects seem to resist meaning, Barthes tells us, which means we have to struggle with their seeming "innocence." We must refuse to be mystified, refuse to take our objects at face value, and probe for their hidden meanings. To understand the real meaning of objects we have to enter "the kitchen of meaning," by which he means we must recognize that objects can't be analyzed as discrete items in an isolated manner, separated from other objects and the society in which they are found.

Meaning is tied, Barthes suggests, to the fact that these objects are signs, which means they are "*constituted by differences*"(1988, 148). This leads him to discuss Ferdinand de Saussure's suggestion that semiotics studies "the life of signs in society," which implies that it will study "systems of objects" (garments, food, images, rituals, protocols, music, and so on).

In addition, Barthes adds, semiotics must study "that mysterious operation by which any message may be impregnated with a secondary meaning, a meaning that is diffuse, generally ideological, and which is known as the '*connoted meaning*'" (1988, 149). Barthes concludes his essay by suggesting that signification has become the dominant concern in the modern world, replacing fact, which used to be "the previously constituted unit of reflection of positivist science" (1988, 149).

De Saussure and the Discovery of Meaning

Since de Saussure's name has played so prominently in the discussion to this point, let me briefly discuss his analysis of how concepts generate meaning. In his *Course in General Linguistics*, published posthumously in 1915, de Saussure points out that language is a social institution and calls for a science to deal with the special nature of language. He writes,

Language is a system of signs that express ideas, and is therefore comparable to a system of writing, the alphabet of deaf-mutes, symbolic rites, polite formulas, military signals, etc. But it is the most important of these systems.

A science that studies the life of signs within society is conceivable; it would be part of social psychology and consequently of general psychology: I shall call it *semiology* (from Greek *sēmeîon*, "sign"). Semiology would show what constitutes signs, what laws govern them. (1915, 16)

Signs, we learn later, are composed of signifiers (sound-images) and signifieds (concepts), and the relation between signifier and signified is arbitrary or based on convention. In recent years the term *semiotics,* which stems from C. S. Peirce's theories, has become dominant and replaced semiology. For our purposes, since both words focus on what signs are and how they function in society, we shall consider them the same thing and use the term semiotics in dealing with signs.

What is important to recognize here is that de Saussure focuses upon the "life of signs in society," pointing out that signs tended to elude individual or social wills (or, from our perspective, analysis). As he puts it, "By studying rites, customs, etc. as signs, I believe that we shall throw new light on the facts and point up the need for including them in a science or semiology and explaining them by its laws" (1915, 17).

De Saussure makes another point that is of great importance. Language, he suggests, "is a system of interdependent terms in which the value of each term results solely from the simultaneous presence of the others." This leads to de Saussure's analysis of concepts: "It is understood that concepts are purely differential and defined not by their positive content but negatively by their relations with the other terms of the system. Their most precise characteristic is in being what the others are not" (1915, 117). Signs function, he tells us, "not through their intrinsic value but through their relative position" (1915, 118). It is relations among signs in a system that is all-important.

This notion has important implications for the study of everyday life. The objects one encounters in everyday life have meaning because they are part of a system and must be understood in that regard. The analogy with language is instructive. Words mean nothing by themselves; it is only in some relationship with other words in a sentence that a word takes on a specific meaning. Barthes had read de Saussure and decided to treat "collective representations" as sign systems, which required, as he pointed out in "The Kitchen of Meaning," that he recognize that the activities and objects he studied had no meaning as isolates but only when they could be related, somehow, to other like phenomena that existed as part of some system of activities and objects.

The Sociologies of Everyday Life

In a book he edited, *Introduction to the Sociologies of Everyday Life*, Jack Douglas brings together a number of sociologists who discuss how their discipline has dealt with everyday life. There are chapters on symbolic interactionism, labeling theory, phenomenological sociology, and existential sociology—all of which represent attempts by sociologists to come to grips with everyday life.

Douglas makes an interesting analogy in his introductory essay:

> Most of our everyday lives are lived in roughly the same way we cook something. That is, there are certain basic rules of cooking (use heat or microwaves to cook) that are almost universally shared and largely unproblematic. There are certain other shared meanings—pepper is hot, for example—and shared paths of action related to these which are not very problematic—always go easy on the pepper. There are also general sets of meanings and rules and paths of action that can be put together in relatively unproblematic ways to make up *recipes for living* in most of the concrete situations in our lives. (1980, 15)

We have to learn how to construct or elicit meanings for the things we do in our everyday lives that are partially problematic, and we pay little or no attention to those aspects of our everyday lives that are unproblematic.

The analogy Douglas uses recalls a fascinating conversation I had with an executive from the Wimpy hamburger chain in England in the early 1970s. I had written an essay on a hamburger I had at a Wimpy's in London and compared it to one I had at a McDonald's in America. This essay appeared in *New Society* and led to an angry letter to the publication by a Wimpy's executive.

I met him and was given a tour of Wimpy's test kitchen and lunch at a Wimpy's. It was one of their standard lunch plates and consisted of a hamburger patty (not on a bun), a hot dog, chutney, and egg. For dessert I had an "American" sundae, which consisted of a scoop of ice cream over which some fruit cocktail had been poured. When I told the executive that I had worked as a soda jerk and that Americans don't usually have sundaes like that, he took offense and told me that Wimpy's had researched the matter.

He mentioned to me, in the course of our conversation, that his wife cooked only seven different main dishes, which he and his family ate week in and week out. This is a rather stark illustration of the way we develop routines that we are comfortable with and tend to follow continually. And the objects we use and the routines (or rituals, if we wish to give these routines somewhat of a sacred flavoring) we follow in which we use these objects are the stuff of everyday life.

These routines or habits can be looked upon as analogous to beliefs, and once they are established, they render it unnecessary to make decisions about what to do in this situation or that. So habits, by doing away with doubt and the need to make decisions, are comforting and reassuring, even though they tend to make life dull, bland, and somewhat boring. But these matters, it turns out, are of great interest and use to historians, as my discussion of the work of Fernand Braudel will show.

History and Material Culture

The first volume of Fernand Braudel's three-volume study of European history is titled *The Structures of Everyday Life: The Limits of the Possible.* An early version was published in France in 1967 with the title *Les structures du quotidien: Le possible et l'impossible.* The French subtitle is slightly different from the English one. The translation I am using is by Sian Reynolds, who translated a revised French version of the books.

In his introduction, Braudel points out that he became interested in a zone of economic activity existing everywhere and in "fantastic" volume underneath the market economy, a zone he calls "material life" or "material civilization." The statistics we have about economic activity in the period between the fifteenth and eighteenth centuries come from the market economy, but beneath this economy was an enormous kind of underground economy that involved perhaps as much as 30 or 40 percent of the gross national product and included barter, exchange of services, moonlighting, doing odd jobs, and that kind of thing. This period, he suggests, represents a kind of transitional phase between the ancient societies that were disintegrating and the new capitalistic societies that were being formed.

On the Definition of Everyday Life

Braudel defines everyday life as the realm of what seems to be the trivial and uninteresting. He writes:

> Everyday life consists of the little things one hardly notices in time and space. The more we reduce the focus of vision,

the more likely we are to find ourselves in the environment of material life: the broad sweep usually corresponds to History with a capital letter, to distant trade routes, and the networks of national or urban economies. If we reduce the length of time observed, we either have the event or the everyday happening. The event is, or is taken to be, unique; the everyday happening is repeated, and the more often it is repeated the more likely it is to become a generality rather than a structure. It pervades society at all levels, and characterizes ways of being and behaving which are perpetuated through endless ages . . . through little details, travellers' notes, a society stands revealed. The ways people eat, dress, or lodge, at the different levels of society, are never a matter of indifference. And these snapshots can also point out contrasts and disparities between one society and another which are not all superficial. (1981, 29)

It is, Braudel suggests, this world of constantly repeated and seemingly insignificant activities and the objects we use in our daily lives (material culture) that is of crucial importance. Everyday life, he suggests, yields insights into history that we have not had before, due to our concentration on important figures and significant events: on kings, parliaments, wars, and that kind of thing. Thus, the second chapter of his book, "Daily Bread," deals with the role played by wheat and other grains in Europe and other countries and gives us a much different perspective on things than we get from conventional historical studies. It is this notion that has informed my book and directed my attention to daily routines.

A great deal depends on the focus we use when approaching history. If we narrow our focus and abandon the grand narratives about the roles of kings and great men and women, we observe a different world. It all depends on what you look for and look at. If we focus on material life, we find the world of the household, the routines that are practiced endlessly and never really noticed. We are not dealing with events in the sense that what we examine is, it would seem at first glance, trivial.

But little things, Braudel tells us at the conclusion of his book, add up. This "dust" of history combines, through indefinite repetition, "to form linked chains. Each of them represents the thousands of others that have crossed the silent depths of time and *endured*" (1981, 560). It is with these chains that Braudel has been concerned; they help him gain a perspective on history, put things into some kind of balance.

Material culture, he adds, changes much more slowly than other aspects of life studied by historians, and it thus provides a base that helps us see transitory events more clearly. He explains why he uses the term "civilization": "Civilizations do indeed create bonds, that is to say an order, bringing together thousands of cultural possessions effectively different from, and at first sight even foreign to, each other—goods that range from those of the spirit and the intellect to the tools and objects of everyday life" (1981, 560).

Bloom's Morning is not a history of everyday life and not a sociology of everyday life in that it does not involve social interactions, people interacting in concrete situations, but it is historical, sociological, and political in that it considers the "social" (in the most profound sense of the term) dimensions of everyday life, of the things we do over and over again, our routines, and the objects we use in following them.

Henri Lefebvre's *Everyday Life in the Modern World*

The Harper Torchbooks paperback edition of Lefebvre's book has a cover that was designed by David November. It shows a table with a checkerboard tablecloth, a bottle of milk, a glass of milk, and a bowl of cereal on it. We also see a wall with a window, and as we look out the window we see an atomic explosion. Thus we find two extremes of life: an utterly banal scene, repeated over and over again in families in America and Western Europe (and perhaps most everywhere in the world now that breakfast cereal is spreading in popularity), and a cataclysmic event suggesting at least the possibility of the destruction of the world.

Lefebvre offers a number of ways of considering everyday life. He points out, for instance, that he has made a conscious decision "to explore *recurrence*. Everyday life is made of recurrences" (1971, 18). He offers a different definition of everyday life a short while later and writes, "Everyday life is sustenance, clothing, furnishing, homes, neighborhoods, environment. . . . Call it material culture if you like, but do not confuse the issue" (1971, 21). He connects everyday life with modernity, "the one crowning and concealing the other, revealing and veiling it. Everyday life, a compound of insignificances united in this concept, responds and corresponds to modernity, a compound of signs by which our society expresses and justifies itself and which forms part of its ideology" (1971, 24). In this respect he differs from Braudel, who sees everyday life as always existing, and not as something brought into being by modernity.

For Lefebvre, these two concepts, everyday life and modernity, enable us to escape from being passive victims of the media. If we tear ourselves away from the immediacy of things and from an attitude of unconcern and the acceptance of things as they are—that is, if we can see the objects and activities that are the stuff of everyday life as *signs*—we can make progress. He writes, "If you allow the swarms of signs to flow over you from television and radio sets, from films and newspapers and ratify the commentaries that determine their meanings, you will become a passive victim of the situation; but insert a distinction or two—for instance everyday life and modernity—and the situation is changed: you are now the active interpreter of signs" (1971, 25). Lefebvre believes this analysis will, among other things, enable us to see the ideological aspects of everyday life that we tend to ignore.

In order to make sense of everyday life, adopting a Saussurean posture, we must have something to counter it and thus help define it, and this concept for Lefebvre is "the festival." He mentions in his discussion his longer work on everyday life, which deals with "Style" and "Festival." He complains that "Style" has become culture, with negative results, and writes, "Style has degenerated into culture—subdivided into everyday culture for the masses and a higher culture, a split that led to specialization and decay. Art can replace neither style nor the Festival, and is an increasingly specialized activity that parodies the Festival, an ornament adorning everyday life but failing to transform it" (1971, 36). But, he adds, "Festival" has not completely disappeared, though the remnants of it that exist are pale imitations of what Festival was and might be, in the right social setting.

Let me offer my own suggestions, at this point, about how Festival helps us understand everyday life as it is currently lived in modern societies. "Festival" can be seen as the opposite of everyday life and thus as that which gives it meaning.

EVERYDAY LIFE	FESTIVAL
routine	special
work	leisure, play, holidays
boredom	excitement
uniformity	difference
continual	sporadic
travel	tourism

Everyday life is the realm of the routine, whereas Festival represents an interruption of this routine in the name of celebration and excitement. In everyday life we spend most of our time at work, while Festival, in its modern manifestations, is devoted to leisure, play, fun. Festival opposes the excitement of special moments (whether during something like Carnival in Rio or New Orleans) to the relatively boring and unexciting aspects of everyday life.

It is in fact everyday life that makes Festival exciting and Festival that makes everyday life what it is. Just as certain head-hunting tribes used to organize their everyday lives around head-hunting expeditions that took place once or twice a year, modern men and women organize their lives around the trips they take when they are on vacation. That explains, in part, why tourism is one of the giant industries of the present day. Travel I define as being in the realm of work, whereas tourism is defined as being in the realm of leisure and play. If all one does is be a tourist, the role loses its definition as the opposite of everyday life and becomes a kind of work.

Lefebvre suggests, in fact, that contemporary societies are in a state of transition and are moving from labor to leisure. There are, he points out, three kinds of time: pledged time (work), free time (leisure), and compulsive time (demands on us other than work, such as commuting), and compulsive time is increasing faster than leisure time. Our lives, it could be said, are being sucked up by the demands of compulsive time, which is part of everyday life.

In the modern world, leisure has lost its festivity and has been absorbed, so to speak, by our consumer culture; leisure has become what Lefebvre calls "a generalized display: television, cinema, tourism" (1971, 54). The most powerful force working on people in this consumer culture is advertising, which is becoming the main ideological instrument of the day, and the ideology it preaches is consumption. Advertising, Lefebvre argues, has replaced the image of the active man, the maker (*Homo faber*) with that of the consumer who has been taught to think he finds happiness in consumption. "To buy [let me take liberties with Berkeley here] is to be perceived" and to feel that one exists. And it is the bills in the mail, later on, that confirm one's continued existence.

What advertising does, and I am compressing Lefebvre's argument greatly here, is to shift the way we perceive the world. We used to make sense of the world, he says, by symbols, "derived from nature but containing definite social implications" (1971, 62). This gave way to what he calls, in his special vocabulary, signs, as we gave greater authority to the written word.

In the modern world there has been another shift—from signs to signals, which can be grouped into codes, and which can be used to control our behavior. We are not very far removed from Pavlov here, except that the signals humans are given are more complicated than the ones Pavlov used. (Lefebvre's definition of signals is basically what de Saussure called a sign, whose meaning is conventional.)

What is important to recognize is that advertising deals essentially with the objects and rituals that use products and that are so important in our everyday lives. Every object we use is something we purchased, and the objects we use in our rituals (whether it be smoking cigarettes or putting on makeup) all come with a host of meanings attached—meanings given to them by advertising. What McLuhan did in *The Mechanical Bride*, among other things, was to analyze the meanings of the objects placed on them by advertising and subject these meanings to analysis.

Lefebvre also believes that advertising is a royal road to the collective unconscious. As he puts it,

Attempts to apprehend everyday life intellectually fail not because it vanishes into the unconscious, but because it collapses. And yet it is signified everywhere: in publicity, in techniques of happiness (or rather satisfaction), organisms and organizations. . . . Desire "desires," and in so far as this term that denotes a state of "being" means anything, desire desires itself, desires its end, its disappearance in a flash of satisfaction. Only the signified is involved in the act of desiring one thing or another, being satisfied by it and finding satisfaction in it; the signifier, as psychoanalysts know, disappears. (1971, 117)

It is desire that advertising stimulates, knowing that it can never be sated, knowing that it can only be quieted for a moment until it is unleashed once again by a print advertisement or radio or television commercial for some product.

De Certeau and *The Practice of Everyday Life*

Michel de Certeau's *The Practice of Everyday Life* was written in 1974, but the English translation by Steven Rendall did not appear until 1984, so for those who don't read French, de Certeau is a relatively late entry in the debate on everyday life. And he brings a perspective to the subject quite different from Lefebvre's and much closer to that of Braudel. De Certeau sees ordinary people leading their everyday lives as being able to subvert the power of governmental agencies, consumer culture, whatever you will, and resist domination and control. He is interested, for example, in the use to which people put the products they purchase—in the kind of production ordinary people carry on with the goods they consume, a production that often is at odds with the "official" imperatives of the society in which they find themselves. The weak, for de Certeau, have found ways of making use of the strong and thus neutralizing, to various extents, the degree to which the strong dominate and control them.

De Certeau makes a distinction between strategy and tactics. A strategy assumes that a place can be set apart for "generating relations with an exterior distinct from it (competitors, adversaries, "clienteles," "targets," or "objects" of research)" (1984, xix). A tactic, unlike a strategy, does not have an institutional or spatial localization and is something that "insinuates itself into the other's place fragmentarily, without taking it over in its entirety, without being able to keep it at a distance" (1984, xix). Tactics do not show themselves but arise on the spur of the moment, manipulate events to make them become opportunities, are fugitive, and are the realm of the weak.

As he describes things,

> Many everyday practices (talking, reading, moving about, shopping, cooking, etc.) are tactical in character. And so are, more generally, many "ways of operating": victories of the "weak" over the "strong" (whether the strength be that of powerful people or the violence of things or of an imposed order, etc.), clever tricks, knowing how to get away with things, "hunter's cunning," maneuvers, polymorphic situations, joyful discoveries, poetic as well as warlike. The Greeks called these "ways of operating" *metis*. But they go much further back, to the immemorial intelligence displayed in the tricks and imitations of plants and fishes. From the depth of the ocean to the streets of modern megalopolises, there is a continuity and permanence in these tactics. (1984, xix)

These practices de Certeau discusses involve the routines con artists use, the deceptions people use in their everyday interactions (of such interest to the ethnomethodologists), and that kind of thing. As an example, he cites a practice known in France as *la perruque*, which means "the wig."

This term, *la perruque*, relates to things workers do for themselves while on the job that they disguise as work for their employer. He offers as an example a secretary who writes a love letter to her boyfriend while at work. She seems to be working for her boss but in reality is doing something for herself. This practice is multiplied a million times over and is all-pervasive in the workday world, an example of the way in which people are able to manipulate things for their own purposes. We develop, de Certeau suggests, a repertory of "tricks," ploys, put-ons, cons (or living by our "wits," so to speak)—tactics by which the weak subvert the strong and manipulate the powerful.

Anyone who has served in the army can probably give numerous examples of the way individuals "subvert" the system of bureaucratic regulation that the army has set up to control people. I served in the army between 1956 and 1958 in Washington, D.C., in the Headquarters Company of the Military District of Washington.

One of the clerks, a corporal, figured out a way to get all of his friends in the Headquarters Company promoted early. One of his duties was to send promotions off to various bases in our military district. He discovered that if he sent surplus promotions to certain bases, they would inevitably be returned, and then these surplus promotions could be awarded to people in the Headquarters Company. (This meant that people in other bases got fewer promotions than they were entitled to, but the moral aspects of subversions are not of great interest to those drafted into the army.) By the time the army got wise to what the clerk was doing, he had only two months of service left. This, I would suggest, is a classic example of *la perruque*, and anyone who has been in the army or dealt with any bureaucracy can probably recount examples of how people have been able to "beat the system," as we would put it in America.

Everyday Life as a Narrative

For de Certeau, everyday life has a narrative structure to it that is important. It is central, he argues, for a theory of practices, and he cites the work of Marcel Detienne in this respect: "Marcel Detienne, who is a historian and an anthropologist, has deliberately chosen to tell stories. . . . He does not assume that behind all these stories, secrets exist whose gradual unveiling would give him, in the background, his own place, that of interpretation. For him, these tales, stories, poems, and treatises are already practices. They say exactly what to do. They constitute an act which they intend to mean" (1984, 80). Stories are functional, we might say (to adopt the language of the sociologist), in that they show people, rather than tell them, what to do and how to do it. He ends his chapter "Story Time" with a quote from Aristotle—who had arrived, de Certeau suggests, at the age of *metis*: "The more solitary and isolated I become, the more I come to like stories."

De Certeau offers us what might be described, literally as well as figuratively, as a "reader response" theory of everyday life, one that places attention on the "role of the reader" and suggests that readers (consumers, ordinary people) play a more important part in the scheme of things than we have given them credit for: that they can resist domination and subvert the powerful. He sees much more freedom for the ordinary person than Lefebvre does, for whom everyday life involves terror and domination.

He explains this "freedom" in his discussion of "The ideology of 'informing' through books":

This image of the "public" is not usually made explicit. It is nonetheless implicit in the "producers" claim to *inform* the population, that is, to "give form" to social practices. Even protests against the vulgarization/vulgarity of the media often depend on an analogous pedagogical claim, inclined to believe that its own cultural models are necessary for the people in order to educate their minds and elevate their hearts, the elite upset about the "low level" of journalism or television always assumes that the public is moulded by the products imposed on it. To assume that is to misunderstand the act of "consumption." This misunderstanding assumes that "assimilating" necessarily means "becoming similar to" what one absorbs and not "making something similar" to what one is, making it one's own, appropriating or reappropriating it. (1984, 166)

What de Certeau is suggesting is that people are not automatically molded by the media—a notion that used to be known as the "hypodermic needle" theory of media, which assumed that people all respond immediately and in the same way to the media to which they are exposed.

De Certeau continues on with his attack on this theory of media, and by implication, consumption in general. He writes, "The idea of producing a society by a 'scriptural system' has continued to have as its corollary the conviction that although the public is more or less resistant, it is moulded by (verbal or iconic) writing, that it becomes similar to what it receives, and that it is *imprinted* by and like the text which was imposed on it" (1984, 167). This text that does the imprinting used to be found at school, but now, de Certeau suggests, "the text is society itself" in its various forms (urbanism, industrialism, television, and so on). The problem with the notion that people are imprinted by the media and the societies in which they find themselves is that it doesn't allow any room for human freedom, for imagination, for creativity, for autonomy, and for resistance.

There are strong similarities between de Certeau's theories of resistance and the notions of reader-response theorists such as Wolfgang Iser, who argues in "The Reading Process: A Phenomenological Approach" that we must consider not only the text itself (that is, the role played by the producer of the text) but also the role played by the reader. Every literary text has, Iser suggests, two poles: an artistic pole and an aesthetic pole. The artistic pole refers to the created work and the role of the author of the text; the aesthetic pole refers to the role the reader/viewer/listener plays. As he puts it, "The work is more than the text, for the text only takes on life when it is realized, and furthermore the realization is by no means independent of the individual disposition of the reader . . . the convergence of text and reader brings the literary work into existence" (Lodge 1988, 212). Thus, literary texts are not works that have only one interpretation and that impose or imprint this interpretation, their "meaning," directly on their readers, and the same can be said for other kinds of texts—namely, those created by the mass media and, by implication, the products of our consumer culture.

People are always "decoding" mass-mediated texts based on their own experiences, their socioeconomic class, educational attainments, and so on, and using them for their own purposes. Things are not as simple as the hypodermic theorists of media (and culture in general) would have us believe. Advertisers run things up flagpoles but not everyone salutes, and even when some do salute, we can't be sure why they are doing so and whether or not they are really serious about what they are doing.

De Certeau argues that people can resist the media, yet he seems to take away with his left hand what he gave us with his right. He calls attention, in his chapter "Believing and Making

People Believe," to another important aspect of the mass media—namely, that their texts are, to a considerable degree, narratives:

> An anonymous code, information innervates and saturates the body politic. From morning to night, narrations constantly haunt streets and buildings. They articulate our existences by teaching us what they must be. They "cover the event," that is to say, they *make* our legends (*legenda*, what is to be read and said) out of it. Captured by the radio (the voice is the law) as soon as he awakens, the listener walks all day long through the forest of narrativities from journalism, advertising, and television, narrativities that still find time, as he is getting ready for bed, to slip a few final messages under the portals of sleep. Ever more than the God told about by theologians of earlier days, these stories have a providential and predestining function: they organize in advance our work, our celebrations, and even our dreams. Social life multiplies the gestures and modes of behavior *(im)printed* by narrative models; it ceasely (sic) reproduced and accumulates "copies" of stories. Our society has become a recited society, in three senses: it is defined by *stories (récits*, the fables constituted by our advertising and informational media), by *citations* of stories, and by the interminable *recitation* of stories. (1984, 186)

These narratives that pervade our existence have a certain kind of power over us, de Certeau suggests, by showing us things we then tend to believe. What we don't see we don't have to believe, he suggests. But what we do see, since "seeing is believing," at least to a certain degree, we must believe. Where we once used to think that there was some important kind or essence of reality hidden behind appearances, we now have capitulated, in some measure, to the power of visual images and what we can see. We have moved from being logocentric to oculocentric, and that has made a big difference.

Of course most of us learn that what we are shown is mediated and based on someone's decision—a television director who commands "show this and not that"—so seeing may be believing, but it is not necessarily believing that one is getting at the truth of the matter. Seeing is selective. Thus, even if images have a power to compel belief, we see images from our own perspective and we tend to question whether what we see is always the whole story.

Even so, de Certeau argues, discussing the thought processes of a person exposed to simulations, "a belief survives that refutation that everything we know about their fabrication makes available to him" (1984, 188). So there is, it would seem, an element of determinacy that can be injected into the situation and a question of to what degree we really are able to resist manipulation by the media. We can, perhaps, rescue de Certeau from the element of determinacy found in his writing about images and reality by suggesting that people look at images selectively and that even images are interpreted in various ways by different people.

As far as narratives are concerned, we learn to "tune them out" a great deal of the time, we misinterpret them other times, and most of us recognize that these narratives that fill the media and our media-dominated lives are constructions often created for particular reasons, so our "invincible ignorance" and our skepticism and cynicism still protect us, to a certain degree, from the power that narratives have over our imaginations and belief systems.

It is here, with de Certeau's focus on narratives, that I would like to leave this argument, for it is a convenient place to begin my study of everyday life, *Bloom's Morning*. I should point out that Bloom's morning is told, first of all, as a story. It deals, in the most elementary way (an example of literary micromini-malism, if you will), with how Bloom spends his morning. It is only after that story that my *explication de texte* begins and I start analyzing Bloom's morning in terms of what his actions and the artifacts he uses suggest about everyday life—for people of a certain gender, class, ethnicity, and so on, in the United States—though I argue, also, that in many respects Bloom is a representative figure, and that in learning about Bloom, by observing how he spends his morning, we also learn a good deal about ourselves.

PART 2
Ulysses Sociologica

Mr. Leopold Bloom ate with relish the inner organs of beasts and fowls. He liked thick giblet soup, nutty gizzards, a stuffed roast heart, liver slices fried with crustcrumbs, fried hencod's roes. Most of all he liked grilled mutton kidneys which gave to his palate a fine tang of faintly scented urine.

—James Joyce, *Ulysses*

O N E

Bloom's Morning

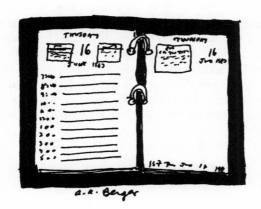

Mr. Leopold Bloom was awakened by the buzzer in his digital clock radio. He was lying in a king-sized bed in the master bedroom of his house. He lay beneath a designer sheet and a comforter, which he tossed aside, and slid out of bed. He was wearing a pair of pajamas. The broadloom carpet in the bedroom felt soft and comfortable. He put on his slippers and went to the closet, where he took out his jogging outfit and got into it. He went for a jog around the neighborhood, returned, got undressed, put on a bathrobe, and ambled over to the bathroom. He took a long, hot, invigorating shower. He loved the smell of the new bath soap he had purchased recently. He shampooed his hair. Then he put on his bathrobe again and dried his hair with an electric hairdryer. Next he brushed his teeth using an electric toothbrush, took a shave, and put on his underwear. Then he put on his stockings, a suit, and his shoes, selected a tie to wear, and went to the kitchen.

There wasn't very much in the refrigerator, so he slipped out of the house and strolled to the local supermarket, where he picked up a few items, and returned home. The morning newspaper had arrived. He made himself a big breakfast: orange juice, cereal, bacon and eggs, coffee, and toast. He put his garbage in the waste disposal, his dirty dishes in the dishwasher, and an empty cereal carton in the trash compactor and heard the pleasant sound of the morning mail being slipped through the front door.

That was Bloom's morning.

T W O

Digital Clock Radios

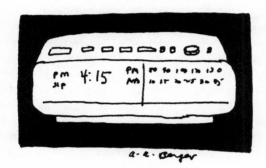

The digital clock radio represents a fusion of the control (and the ultimate dissolution) of time and of entertainment. It is at face value a combination of a digital clock and a radio, but I think it is much more than the sum of its parts.

A digital clock differs from an analog clock in significant ways. Analog clocks (and analog watches, with their sweeping hands and dials) suggest that time is continuous. We can situate ourselves in time and feel a sense of connectedness with both the past and the future. So many minutes have already passed, so many more must pass before a given hour is reached. The very organization of the analog clock suggests relatedness. We can visually sense where we are in relation to the passage of time, which is why some analog watches don't even have numbers. This sense of relatedness does not hold for the digital clock.

The digital clock merely produces numbers that locate us in the immediate present, but it also, at the same time, disconnects us from the past and the future. A digital clock destroys time as we traditionally think of it; time is dissolved into an endless succession of discrete and unrelated moments.

This dissolution of time, the radical separation of an instant of time from both time past and time future, can be looked upon as a metaphor for the alienation many people feel in contemporary society. Our electronic culture gives us precision at the cost of community and a sense of relatedness. Thus digital clocks are objects that reflect, it can be argued, the alienation many people now feel. These clocks are both symptoms of this alienation and perpetrators of it, for their very accuracy is, in certain respects, upsetting and in some ways even dehumanizing.

Clocks are, we must remember, whatever else they may be, instruments of control. We lived for centuries without them. The first clocks appeared in the thirteenth century; minute hands appeared in the seventeenth century (with the invention of the pendulum), and the second hand had to wait until the eighteenth century. These early clocks revolutionized people's lives, for until the development of clocks it was not possible to regulate the way people spent their time with very much accuracy. The clock made possible the development of the industrial era. People learned, eventually, that "time is money." Given this, time suddenly becomes a precious commodity.

And the more accuracy we have at our command, the better things are—as far as utilizing clocks as instruments of control is concerned. To be middle class means, among other things, to be socialized into getting places on time, into internalizing the correct attitude toward time.

The digital clock represents the final stage of the clock, which has evolved from being a mechanical to an electromechanical to an electronic device. These devices offer us incredible accuracy (which can be translated into meaning even more rigorous domination), but, ironically, they also involve the dissolution of time as we traditionally understand it—that is, time as duration. The second hand, as it slowly sweeps around the face of an analog clock, reminds us of the continuity of time . . . seconds follow one another, as do minutes and hours, until everything starts over again.

But time is atomized with the digital clock, broken into discrete moments that are suddenly revealed to us second by second, minute by minute. Time becomes a succession of presents and nothing more. If our lives took on something of the regularity of mechanical clocks in earlier times and became like clockwork, what will happen to us in the age of electronic clocks? There is, I suggest, a relationship between the psychological imperatives of the digital clock, which I have just spelled out, and the alienation, sense of isolation, and sense of powerlessness and futility that many people feel in contemporary society. The digital clock is, in its own way, a supreme example of hyperindividualism, of egocentrism, of narcissism and self-concern.

Now this powerful device has been merged with the radio and can be found in the bedrooms of countless millions of people. The digital clock radio combines control and entertainment, merging two phenomena—the clock and a medium of entertainment, the radio, which is itself a complicated and interesting phenomenon.

The typical digital clock radio has an alarm clock function: One can wake up with a buzzer or by having a radio station turned on. (The digital clock radio even offers what seems to be a bit of humanity . . . usually it has a snooze-alarm button that enables one to doze for a few minutes or so before the alarm or radio comes on again. This is supposed to mitigate the horror of having to get up and face the world.)

And what is the content of the radio programs many people listen to? News programs containing frequent time alerts, to make certain listeners do not slack off, and advertisements of products of our consumer culture (which are the inducements for going to work in the first place). Sandwiched in between the time alerts and commercials is news—records of the disasters and tragedies of the night before, along with weather reports, scores from the various athletic competitions of the previous day or night, reports on traffic jams, and various other kinds of chitchat.

Most radio programming, I would suggest, is also involved with controlling us—reminding us, endlessly, of the time (so we get to work on time and make money) and urging us to buy certain products (so we know what to spend our money on). As far as radio is concerned, the most precious thing we can give to it is time . . . and there is great competition between radio stations to control "drive time," the time commuters spend in their automobiles going to and from work.

In the newest-model cars, the clocks are now—of course—all digital. The clock is an important coordinating device and cannot be dispensed with. The question we must ask ourselves is, To what degree do we control our clocks and to what degree are we dominated by them? Is it possible that the digital clock radio is not the innocuous, friendly little device we thought it was (because of its snooze alarm) but is really a tyrant that, allied with radio and the imperatives generated by entertainment tied to this medium, has an insidious power to shape our lives? We may set our digital alarm clock radios, but they shape our lives.

THREE

King-Sized Beds

The king-sized bed represents, in one sense, the democratization of kingship. Once, kings were seen to be something special . . . we thought "divinity doth hedge a king." They reigned and ruled (unlike Queen Elizabeth, who reigns but does not rule either her family or her kingdom, so it seems) and were persons of some consequence. Nowadays, any peasant with a couple hundred dollars can buy a king-sized bed and sleep, so one would imagine, the way kings do. Kings, like dogs and horses, are judged by the quality of their bloodlines. Like bulls, kings are evaluated now chiefly in terms of their breeding potentialities.

45

King-Sized Beds

There are, it turns out, two different sizes for king-sized beds: The regular king-sized bed is 76 inches by 80 inches, and the West Coast king-sized bed is 72 inches by 84 inches. I learned this from the Sears catalogue (no longer published), which informs us that residents of Arizona, California, Hawaii, Nevada, and Utah can only order the West Coast version of the king-sized bed. In either case one gets a bed that is approximately 6,000 square inches—in contrast to the full-sized bed, which is about 4,000 square inches, and the queen-sized bed, which is 4,800 square inches.

We also learn from the king-sized bed (and other king-sized objects) that, somehow, kings are associated with size and that kings are "big." That is, if king-sized beds are big, then kings must be big. We know from history, and from the few kings who are around now, that not all kings are big physically. So they must be big in some other way—namely psychologically.

The term "king" is connected, interestingly enough, with the term "father." Kings are father figures . . . Otto Rank, in his essay "The Myth of the Birth of the Hero," writes that we find "the use of identical words for king and father, in the Indo-Germanic languages (compare the German *Landesvater*, father of his country—king)." Now when we sleep on a king-sized mattress we are, in complicated ways, becoming kings ourselves . . . and perhaps even more important, replacing former kings who slept in such beds. I'm suggesting that although we are not aware of the full psychological significance of what we are doing, sleeping in a king-sized bed is connected with Oedipal matters, simple and complex.

With the king-sized bed we have finally "made it" into our father's bed, where we can make love to the queen . . . even if it is a substitute queen we find there. King-sized beds are, then, intimately connected to yearnings for power and domination in our psyches . . . and to residues from our Oedipus complexes, which are the ultimate source of these strivings. We become the kings of our minikingdoms . . . our six-thousand-square-inch domains.

Ironically, we are, relatively speaking, smaller in king-sized beds than we are in full- or queen-sized beds. We take up less of the bed. Thus, ultimately, our fathers have their revenge, for when we finally get to take their place in bed—get to fill their shoes, so to speak—we find that we are, somehow, *smaller* than we thought we were. Our fathers' shoes and beds are too big for us.

The king-sized bed also represents, to move into another area, a general tendency found in modern society to make gradations in everything. There are variations in size, weight, strength, and cost in most of the products in our consumer culture. And this may lead to the sense of relative deprivation that so many people feel, for although they have a great deal, they often don't have the newest, brightest, or king-sized versions of things that others have. They live, then, under a cloud of despair and desperation caused by a sense of relative deprivation. To have a bed is not enough nowadays. One must have a king-sized bed (or whatever); otherwise, we feel we have somehow failed.

Of course a king-sized bed implies a huge "master" bedroom, so that the bed doesn't seem too much out of scale. And that implies a large house so the bedroom doesn't take up too much of the house. And the large house implies many possessions, so you don't feel as if you are living in an empty barn. Thus, one is plunged into a whole set of interrelated needs generated by or revolving around the first purchase, the king-sized bed.

There is another psychological penalty connected with the king-sized bed: You are far away from your sleeping partner. There is a kind of separation, perhaps even alienation, implied here. Yes, one is more comfortable, one can twist and turn without bothering one's partner . . . but one also is further removed from physical contact, from body heat, from the actual touch of one's partner. We are just one step away from each partner having his or her own bed.

The king-sized bed may be an attempt to attain the comfort and privacy of separate beds and yet keep, somehow, the symbolic significance of the double bed. We do this by combining two single beds and making a huge double bed that is so large you can "escape" your partner even though you're in the same bed. Proxemically speaking, one has moved from intimate space to something close to social or public space.

I'm not sure whether the king-sized bed is a sign of estrangement (unconscious as it may be) or a cause of estrangement . . . or whether these beds both cause and reinforce this psychological separation. It may even be, in some cases, good for husbands and wives to "disengage" somewhat. Maybe ambiguity and ambivalence are what is significant about the king-sized bed: You can be separate and yet joined at the same time, enjoying, then, the best of both worlds . . . and not having to pay the penalty for being part of either.

F O U R

Sheets

Sheets are physically thin, but psychologically they are "deep." We learn this from Roland Barthes, who explained in *Mythologies* that if a detergent can clean "deeply," then the linen that it cleans must also be deep—an insight that advertising agencies provide us with and one that had escaped people before this matter was called to their attention, indirectly, by advertising agencies.

One lies on sheets physically, but psychologically one is "in" them. Actually, we generally sleep *between* sheets, so that they form a kind of barrier that separates and protects us—from our comforters and from mattresses. (If sheets are deep, imagine what mattresses are—psychologically speaking, that is.)

Sheets—which I am taking as a preeminent example of a whole genre of artifacts, namely linen—have recently become objects of art, and there are many different brands of designer-styled sheets. Gone is the old functionality of the white sheet and the association of whiteness with cleanness . . . and purity. White was a kind of absolute that enabled people to estimate how clean their sheets were. One could compare whitenesses, and soap companies could claim that their products produced "whiter" whites than other brands of soaps did. With the designer sheet, full of colors and designs, the old absolute is gone and sheets can be clean, but this is not connected with their whiteness. We have now been forced to redefine what we mean by a clean sheet. And cleanliness, per se, may no longer be as important as it once was, when sheets were white and called forth associations with hospitals and asepsis.

Our sheets no longer have the immediate function of protecting us from something else . . . whether it be germs or dirt or whatever. Instead, they now provide a kind of aesthetic experience. It may be more important, actually, for sheets to be beautiful than clean. When we sleep on designer sheets we benefit psychologically by feeling that we have done as much as we could to enrich and ennoble our lives, that we have replaced functionality whenever possible with beauty.

There is, of course, no reason why a beautiful object—like a designer's sheet—can't also be functional: made of good material, constructed well, for example, and in many cases that is the situation. Sheets are (or were) humble objects, yet they have always been able to signify a great deal. Silk sheets signify luxury. According to legend, Madame Chiang Kai-shek, when a student at Wellesley (or wherever), slept only on silk sheets—and they were changed every day. One can only imagine what it is like to sleep on a silk sheet . . . the absolute smoothness, the luxuriance. But perhaps also the discomfort . . . since silk sheets are not as absorbent as cotton. The all-cotton sheet has been replaced by sheets that contain some manmade fibers and that do not need ironing (though there are many who still insist upon all-cotton sheets).

But one pays a price . . . for these sheets with manmade fibers are not as absorbent or comfortable as all-cotton sheets. Heavy muslin cotton sheets seem almost to be like boards—starched and stiff, they function as a kind of armor. They are coarse, thick, unyielding . . . not what most people want in their sheets. Look at how Sears describes some of its sheets: "Indulge yourself in the smooth softness of these crisp, cool sheets. Your bed will be a fashionable and enticing retreat once you dress it in these exciting colors, patterns and designs." We want "softness" yet "crispness" in our sheets. That is, we want to be succored and also to feel that our sheets are clean and refreshing. Sheets, then, have been made to bear a heavy burden—psychologically as well as physically.

Once we liberated sheets from being white and thus changed our bedrooms from being hospital wards to anything else we wanted them to be, we were able to indulge in all kinds of fantasies: the garden (of Eden), the geometric universe, the world of comic-strip superheroes, and so on. Our view of sex changed at the same time . . . it became more aesthetic, more recreational. One has now what might be called "designer sex" in between designer sheets.

Designer sheets also do a better job of protecting us, psychologically, from "dirt" and other forms of pollution and such. One thing sheets do is absorb blood, semen, and sweat. On white sheets these discharges have a starkness and reality that is discomforting. On designer sheets, one doesn't notice them as much. They become lost in the artwork, so to speak, and are less apparent, less distressing. That may be why "whiteness" was so crucial with the traditional white sheet . . . when laun-

dered and "white," the sheet erased evidence of bodily functions and enabled us to escape, for a brief period, anxiety about our bodies and bodily processes.

The development of the designer sheet is probably connected to changes going on in society and the evolution of ideas about the body, body fluids, and sex. The birth control pill probably was most instrumental in changing attitudes about sex . . . and the designer sheet merely was part of the whole process of change. But the designer sheet does play an important role in reinforcing and making more permanent the changes in values and attitudes brought on by the pill . . . and other technological advances, such as the French birth control pill and the development of condoms for women.

In addition to the aesthetic aspects of designer sheets, there are other factors to be considered. On the psychological level, the smell of the newly laundered sheet augments the positive feelings we get from sheets. And on the economic level, designer sheets are very profitable for merchandisers and the actual designers of these sheets, as well. To assume that designer sheets are only one more example of economic exploitation by manufacturers and retailers is to miss the profound psychological significance of these objects.

F I V E

Comforters

a-a- Berger

The comforter has replaced the electric blanket in "modern" homes as the correct means of keeping oneself warm. The electric blanket was a giant step forward from old-fashioned woolen blankets, which were heavy and inhibited body movement. (The same applies to quilts and all the other old technologies used to keep people warm at night.) One paid a price for being warm—a kind of relentless weight that practically immobilized you.

This necessity was replaced by the electric blanket, which broke the old equation: weight equals warmth. For thanks to the magic of electricity, one could be warm, even hot, depending upon how you set your controls, and yet feel no weight. (We now have fears that the electric current carried by these blankets and other electronic devices may be bad for us, but that is another matter.)

Thus the electric blanket represented a double liberation for the body . . . from cold and from weight. A rather flimsy little blanket with wires running through it could magically provide heat. But for many people electric blankets are troubling: They fear being electrocuted or that the blanket will start fires. And these fears are not completely groundless, though the number of electrocutions and fires started by electric blankets is statistically insignificant.

Nevertheless, one must exercise a certain amount of care when using an electric blanket, and there are a number of "do's" and "don'ts" of which one must be mindful. You should not put heavy objects, like books, on electric blankets, and you should not leave them on when you aren't in bed, and you shouldn't tuck them in the bottom of your bed (lest they create hot spots), and so on. In return one is promised "gentle warmth."

All of the prohibitions and complications (and newly recognized dangers) involved in using electric blankets can be forgotten when you use a down comforter (or fiberfill variation on that theme). The genius of the comforter is that it is light yet provides great warmth; thus it does everything the electric blanket does but it comes with no complicated rules about usage. One need not worry about electricity and the anxiety that is always generated by its use.

What the down comforter—the finest and most expensive example of the species—represents is something a step beyond manmade science, namely what might be called "natural technology." Comforters use the special characteristics of down to "trap" heat and thus do not need to generate heat. The heat the body gives off is contained and used to keep one warm. It is wonderfully economical.

In essence we are imitating birds and, in fact, exploiting them. The best down comes from geese, and a down comforter is the product of huge amounts of down taken from geese. We're taking a good idea from nature and using it for our own purposes. The "natural," I should point out, is a basic American value: It may be the central value in the American belief system (in contrast to our notion that Europe and other societies represent history and culture, or, for instance, the un-natural). How strange, then, that comforters were popular in Europe well before they became popular in America.

One reason for the rise in popularity of the comforter is that it is, in the long run, an economical way of keeping warm. When electricity was cheap in America, the cost of running an electric blanket was of no concern to us. But as the cost of electricity has risen, we've started looking for ways of economizing—in all aspects of our lives. Thus the comforter not only frees us from the anxiety of using an electric blanket, it also is economical.

The comforter can be looked upon as a sign of a new awareness on the part of many Americans about the need to economize, on the individual level and on the societal one as well. Here I'm thinking about ecological concerns . . . and the fear many people have that we are squandering our resources. Whether this is true is another matter. Many people believe it to be true, and that is what is crucial.

Why the term "comforter"? Comfort suggests many different things: consolation, ease, relief, satisfaction. The word, literally speaking, has to do with strength and power. (*Fort* in French means "strong.") Although the notion of strength may seem far removed from that of the comforter, in fact the association is both close and correct. For what we love about our comforters is the fact that they are powerful objects. They seem at first glance to be rather inert and inconsequential, but in their sphere of action, keeping people warm by capturing their body heat and not letting it dissipate into the atmosphere, they are extremely powerful artifacts.

Their kind of power is the kind we like best in America— power that doesn't call attention to itself, power that is hidden beneath the commonest of appearances (just as Superman's powers were hidden beneath the surface, as reflected in the bumbling Clark Kent). The comforter reflects a kind of democratic power . . . common, ordinary, unassuming, and natural. The comforter reassures us, as we sleep under it, that like it, we are powerful though we may not seem to be. Power comes from naturalness, controlling nature's forces, developing our natural capacities, and so on. In America, a land "without history," as Emerson put it, a land without hereditary aristocracies or royalty, we believe we can be whatever we want—if we have sufficient willpower.

The common man in America who sleeps under a comforter rises in the morning "comforted" (by osmosis) and ready to conquer the world. He has not been burdened by heavy woolen blankets (read here the "dead weight of tradition") or constrained by the requirements of dealing with electricity. The comforter may be an artifact that developed in Europe, but it reflects, beautifully, American ideals and aspirations.

SIX

The Master Bedroom

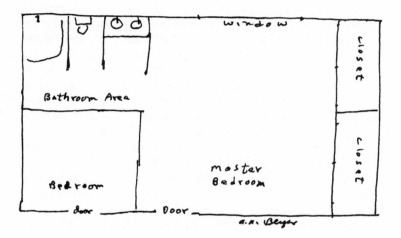

Most new homes, especially those in the suburbs, come with what is known as a "master bedroom suite." This is a fancy way of saying a bedroom that is directly connected to its own bathroom . . . or, in essence, what you get when you rent a room in a hotel. The master bedroom seems anomalous in America, for we regard ourselves as an egalitarian society. Do we not believe it a self-evident truth that "all men are created equal"? Yet the term "master" implies hierarchical relationships and male dominance, among other things.

We can only have masters if we have servants or slaves or subordinates—people who are, one way or another, subservient to masters. This role is all too frequently assumed by the "mistress" of the household, the master's wife, who is given the household as her sphere of dominance. Thus there is an element of sexism connected to the concept of the master bedroom. This phrase also points, rather directly, to the fact that a family is, among other things, a political entity in which there is generally an unequal distribution of power and authority. The master bedroom is, we might say, politically incorrect.

An old Chinese proverb expresses the problematical aspects of family politics beautifully: "It is more difficult to rule a family than an army." That is because in an army there is an obvious and direct chain of command that is maintained by force . . . a hierarchy that makes no claims to being democratic, though it does suggest that hierarchy is both necessary and fair. Families are different. There are no obvious and overt signs of rank, and once children get older and bigger (the son is often taller and bigger than the father-master) physical power is no longer efficacious or practical.

Adolescence, then, from this point of view, is a doubly trying stage, for the adolescent is trying to get control of his or her internal forces and at the same time is involved in a power struggle in his or her family—with parents and perhaps also with siblings. In this stage of family life, frequently the only power the master has is control of the family purse and, for a while, the keys to the car. Families are often "battlegrounds" in which contending forces struggle . . . except that the reasons for the battles are often not clear and the means of determining who has triumphed are vague. In truth, there are no real or permanent triumphs, for the vanquished remain to battle on.

Sociologists and psychologists who have studied families as "power structures" have concluded that generally the power in a typical family is distributed as follows: The children are most powerful, the wife is in second place, and the "master" is in third place because, generally, willpower and determination triumph in family relationships, not overt physical power or even control of family resources.

From this perspective, the "master" is an ironic figure. The American male, once married and with a family, is weak. This is a convention found in our mass media . . . where father seldom knows best . . . when he knows anything at all. Think, for example, of Dagwood Bumstead or of the Simpsons! To marry, then, is to weaken oneself a good deal. But to have children is a disaster as far as power is concerned. (This loss of power may be the reason why so many young people don't wish to get married, even though they may have a child or two, and why those who do get married often decide not to have children.)

It is often the case, then, that only in the outside business world does our "master" have any power. There, where power relationships are clear and authority meaningful, he may be a force to be reckoned with. On the job, the master, especially if he is a professional man, is just that. How painful it must be for so many men to leave this domain and return to that of the family, where a man is, at best, just one of many contending for power and control. The American male often finds himself in a kind of schizophrenic situation, where his sense of self, of accomplishment, of power must be abandoned when he leaves his workplace and returns home.

He may be master outside of the home, but he is, all too often, the servant inside the home. Given this situation, the master bedroom takes on a somewhat different significance—it becomes a place for privacy, for escape, for refuge. It is like having a hotel suite inside one's own home . . . away from others, separate, perhaps even with a sense of anonymity and freedom.

The master bedroom is generally a large room that is luxuriously appointed with broadloom carpeting, chests of drawers, closets, and, of course, direct access to a private bathroom.

Access to a private bathroom is a sign of status in the American corporate world, which has been carried over to the American home. In the master bedroom suite, the American male can peruse his personal treasure—his suits, his shirts, his ties, his shoes, his personal artifacts. He can recall his sexual triumphs and try to forget his sexual disasters. He can watch television, he can relax.

But outside the master bedroom are the kitchen and dining room and living room, where the rest of his family may be found, and where the interfamilial political skirmishes, engagements, and battles remain to be fought. Outside is the world of contending desires and wishes, of the power struggle that is found in all families, in all human relationships. Ironically, the typical American male in his master bedroom is only "master" when he is alone in it. And that is why wealthy families often send their children off to boarding schools as soon as they can. That way, you can turn your whole house into a master bedroom. For the middle-class male who cannot afford this luxury, the master bedroom remains, in many cases, the only place of mastery, repose, and solace.

S E V E N

Closets

In every *Fibber McGee and Molly* program (a popular radio comedy series in days long gone by) there was a scene in which Molly inadvertently opened a closet. "Don't open that closet, Molly," Fibber would plead . . . but it was usually too late. Then there would be a minute devoted to sound effects representing the contents of the closet spilling out.

The closet in this program was an exaggerated version of closets found in many American homes . . . where the endless battle of order and organization against chaos is eternally waged. With rare exceptions, closets are in considerable disarray and almost always in the process of being cleaned up and made orderly.

We fill our closets with clothes, shoes, hair dryers, irons, and gadgets, among other things. What is problematical is that closets are always too small—even when we have huge, room-sized closets. They are too small because we have, it seems, a genius for collecting things and keeping them. Clothes, after all, go out of style every year or so . . . but they come back in style again later on. Thus we keep clothes because we are aware of this cycling process. And the objects we own are not simply objects but reflections of our personalities.

Thus there is a dilemma we all face, caused by the fact that our appetites, our desires, our needs are always infinite and closet space is always finite. The closet becomes the sign, then, of this imbalance. The genius of the closet is that it comes with doors, which allows us to cover up our messes. The closet door enables us to present the appearance of order and control that masks the reality of chaos and disorganization.

The messy closet is a metaphor for our lives and psychological states . . . and our closets are probably pretty accurate reflections of our psyches. We know from work by psychologists that our minds do not function in an orderly manner all the time but race back and forward in time, and that we spend a good deal of time daydreaming and having fantasies. We see this kind of behavior reflected in stream-of-consciousness passages in novels such as *Ulysses*. So it would be relatively normal to have a somewhat messy closet. And in fact, a supremely neat, tightly organized, completely rationalized closet might be an indicator of a rather rigid, slightly "anal" personality. Or that we've employed a closet organizer to come and straighten our closets up for us.

In his essay "Character and Anal Eroticism" (1963) Freud suggested that anal erotics tend to be "exceptionally orderly, parsimonious and obstinate." He describes the orderly person as one characterized by "both bodily cleanliness and reliability and conscientiousness in the performance of petty duties: the opposite would be 'untidy' and 'negligent.'" The situation becomes complicated because in some instances a kind of reversal takes place, what Freud called a "reaction formation," so orderly people as well as messy ones can be anal. Psychoanalytic theory, we find, can get you—literally—coming and going.

But exaggeratedly neat and tidy closets are few and far between. There are, of course, companies that sell closet space-saving systems, which enable a person to make best use of the space available in a given closet. And most closets, no doubt, can be made more efficient. But such triumphs are, I suggest, always only temporary. For as soon as one "rationalizes" a closet and makes it able to accommodate more goods, one then gets more things to jam into the closet, so the space-saving devices are ultimately self-defeating. And this is as it should be. For we keep on changing, keep on purchasing new clothes and new gadgets. A messy closet, bulging with things, is a signifier of a person who is continually changing and evolving. A supremely neat and orderly closet may signify stasis.

Now, it might be argued that it is not the neat, tidy, clean closet that signifies an element of anality, but just the opposite. If one didn't keep everything there would be plenty of room in closets. Closets get full the way they do, this argument goes, because people are collectors and have anal traits—they don't want to let go of anything they have, they are too retentive. I don't think this interpretation is always correct . . . for the emphasis in some cases should be put on the acquisition of things, not on the retention of them. The anal personality is too parsimonious in the first place to spend money and get things, so his or her closet is no problem. And being parsimonious, the anal personality doesn't get rid of things, either.

Ultimately, I think we feel ambivalent about messy closets because we feel ambivalent about order and disorder. As Mary

Douglas writes in *Purity and Danger,* "Order implies restriction; from all possible materials, a limited selection has been made and from all possible relations a limited set has been used. So disorder by implication is unlimited, no pattern has been realized in it, but its potential for patterning is indefinite." This disorder then suggests potentiality and, as Douglas puts it, "symbolizes both danger and power" (1966, 94).

The disorderly and chaotic closet is, then, a signifier of an approach toward experience. Closets are signs that reflect a sense of our possibilities, personalities, and many other things. Our closets are like us—hidden behind the door (read here behind the "mask" of personality) is the real us. This explains why so many people described as "neat" (meaning good, delightful, interesting) are really slobs. It has been said that no man is a hero to his valet. Why? Because valets know, all too well, what their masters' closets are really like.

EIGHT

Jogging

a-a-Berger

Jogging has become a national craze in recent years. It seemed as if we went almost overnight from being a country full of flabby and slovenly souls to a nation of joggers . . . running up and down hills with pained expressions on our faces and feelings of satisfaction and even triumph. Of course, not everyone jogs, and the phenomenon does not affect every social class equally. But certainly something seems to have happened to generate so many joggers.

How can one account for the transformation? I would suggest that a number of things conspired to turn so many Americans into joggers. For one thing, jogging enables people to wear sports uniforms—a pleasure that used to be denied to all except those who have been on high school or college sports teams. There are jogging suits, often designed by "name" designers, and, best of all, there are countless kinds of jogging shoes that one can purchase.

Thus, we can engage in exhaustive research on jogging shoes in the various running magazines and show discrimination by choosing the right brand and model of running shoe. Furthermore, the technology in running shoes is always progressing, so one can cater to a desire to be in the vanguard, at the cutting edge of running-shoe high technology.

In addition to the joy of "getting into uniform," which is a sign to all the world that one is an athlete, there is the matter of righteous sweat that one experiences while jogging. The average middle-class male who jogs probably is a white-collar worker or someone in the information society who does not have a job that generates sweat from physical work. He may sweat, but that sweat will generally be the result of nervous anxiety, which is not the right kind of sweat.

Sweat from jogging is "hard work" sweat, the right kind. For this sweat, we believe, renews the body, eases us out of our tensions and anxieties, and is therapeutic. When we jog we are, in a sense, working—but it is a different kind of work we are doing. We are working "out," and by doing so ridding ourselves of mental and physical poisons. So sweat from jogging is a sign of virtue—a signifier of a healthy body that houses (we would like to think) a healthy mind. For many people in the upper classes, jogging provides the only opportunity they have to sweat from physical exertion and thus be like "ordinary" people.

If you look at people who are jogging, you notice that usually they do not seem to be happy about what they are doing. With good reason. Jogging is, after all, hard work, and it is boring. In addition, dedicated joggers feel they must run all the time and thus often have to run in terrible weather. So there is often a high level of discomfort, if not pain, connected to jogging. But in America, and this is probably a lingering trace of our Puritan heritage, we believe that if something is unpleasant it usually or probably is good for you. Thus, the more pain we experience when we jog, the better we feel about it since we equate the discomfort with benefits: good health, a good feeling about oneself, enough ego strength to look out for one's body, and that kind of thing.

There's probably an element of truth to all this, too. The fact that we have become health-conscious and are now concerned about our bodies is a positive thing. Most of us now recognize that we must devote some time and effort to our physical well-being and that there is a connection between our physical health and our mental health. Thus, the fact that we make time for our bodily well-being is a good thing.

Jogging also has a social dimension to it. If one jogs at a track, one sees various people over and over again and occasionally chats with them. (Tracks are good places to pick up members of the opposite sex . . . or even the same sex, depending upon one's sexual preferences.) If one jogs on trails and running paths, or even through streets in the neighborhood, there is a chance to see people and to explore more thoroughly different sections of town. If one runs where one lives, there is a surveillance function to jogging. You can see who's around and make sure that nothing untoward is going on.

One important aspect of jogging is that it is noncompetitive. There are, of course, some very famous runs that joggers flock to. In San Francisco, for instance, there is the Bay-to-Breakers race that attracts tens of thousands of people, but aside from a handful of serious runners who compete to win in such events, most joggers enter the races only with a desire to complete the run. So one really only competes with oneself. By jogging, one

can "participate in history" (or at least historical runs) and gain a sense of accomplishment.

In jogging, achievement, one of the core American values, is possible without competitiveness. The jogger can compete with himself or herself, as far as speed or endurance is concerned, but this is not real competition. Jogging, then, reflects a considerably different sensibility than running does.

Jogging tells us a good deal about ourselves and suggests that considerable changes seem to have taken place in American society. For example, we may be in the process of modifying and weakening our need for achievement. There may be more to jogging—to running around in circles or going no place in particular at a fast pace (or a not-so-fast pace)—than meets the eye.

N I N E

The Bathrobe

The bathrobe is really ill named, since people tend to take showers rather than baths nowadays. It is a garment that one wears over pajamas or other sleepwear when going to the bathroom, which also is not a particularly accurate term. We wear bathrobes to bathrooms, where we take showers.

Bathrobes are mediating garments; they occupy a slot in between sleepwear (pajamas and the like) and workwear (suits, dresses, and so on). Their function is to facilitate the transition from sleep and the world of ease and relaxation to the world of work and responsibility. They are part of the ritual of getting up and going off to work.

It may seem rather strange to wear a special garment to the bathroom, especially if the bathroom is located in a master bedroom suite. Why bother? Because, I would suggest, the bathrobe has a psychological importance, a sacred significance.

After we have showered and cleansed ourselves, the bathrobe protects us and "consolidates," so to speak, our newly achieved state of grace. Wearing a robe returns us, psychologically, to the days of the early Christians. (That's what they wear in the movies.) The situation is even better if our robe is hooded, as many robes are.

For a moment, we are transported back in time just as, after our showers, we are returned to the state of grace we lived in before we sinned. Thus, there is a rebirth and renewal connected with wearing robes. But there is also a reflection of a sense of guilt, for all clothes are connected to our fall from grace. We wore no clothes in the Garden of Eden when we lived in "primitive innocence" before "the Fall."

Aside from its religious significance (an aspect of the bathrobe that is camouflaged, not apparent to people), the bathrobe is also connected with ease and leisure. Bathrobes are generally made of soft and sometimes luxurious material: velour, terry cloth, and so on. They are not formfitting and don't come with buttons or zippers (which suggest containment and control). We keep bathrobes closed with sashes, very simple and primitive devices.

We wear bathrobes, supposedly, to keep ourselves warm after we've bathed. But many come in knee-length versions, which do not seem to be particularly practical. There is also an ankle-length version, but that type has a drawback in that it impedes easy movement. It does, however, do a good job of covering us.

But why be covered up in one's master bedroom? Or in the kitchen, should one want to wear the bathrobe to breakfast and put off getting dressed in regular clothes as long as possible? Why aren't pajamas adequate for the breakfast table?

It may have something to do with our anxiety and perhaps even sense of shame about our bodies and with our desire to shield them (in particular our genitals) from observation by others. Even with our spouses and children we must keep our "private parts" covered and prevent, to the extent we can, our bodies from being scrutinized.

The bathrobe offers, then, an added layer of protection. It is a more social garment than the pajama or nightgown, which are too revealing. And, of course, bathrobes are meant to keep us warm after our showers and prevent sudden chills and that kind of thing.

There is an element of desexualization or perhaps prudery found in the bathrobe. It is not designed to flatter the body but rather to deemphasize secondary sexual characteristics. Mornings are not meant for sexual activity in America, so the bathrobe does not flatter the female body (thus preventing males from getting sexually excited), nor does it flatter the male body. It is an asexual garment. And the heavier the material of the bathrobe, the more it desexualizes those wearing it, deemphasizing their sexuality.

The bathrobe is one of the few garments that comes in immediate contact with our skin. We wear bathrobes over pajamas before we bathe, but we generally do not put on our pajamas after we bathe. Thus, for a short period, bathrobes touch our skin. (This honor is mostly reserved for our underwear and stockings, which are our primary mediating garments and are used to protect our sexual zones and other areas.)

So our bathrobes seem to have a unique status and responsibility: They must protect us and help us keep our sense of cleanliness and purity, yet they must be heavy enough to keep us warm. And they must prepare us, psychologically, for the "real" world, where, in our suits and suites, we battle with others and

The Bathrobe

demonstrate our power. The bathrobe is a domestic garment that is part of our ritual of getting up and getting ready for the outside world, the world of work, where most of our energies are expended and satisfactions achieved.

T E N

Bathrooms

arthur asa Berger

The bathroom is the place in our homes where we encounter our bodies most directly. It is in the bathroom, a euphemism for toilet, that we urinate and defecate, where body wastes are disposed of. We also cut our nails, shave, and deal with athlete's foot, skin rashes, and underarm odors there. If we can divide our world into sacred and profane realms, the bathroom is certainly profane. But not completely.

We have learned, in our culture, to ignore bodily functions, to put them out of mind as much as possible. There is even a kind of revulsion toward the body and bodily processes such as elimination and perspiring. (As an extreme example, one of the church fathers in the Middle Ages, I believe, described women as "a temple over a sewer.") Most of us probably have an ambivalent feeling toward our bodies, a combination of love and disgust, which manifests itself in different ways.

And the bathroom reflects this, for if it is a chamber in which we come to grips with body processes most directly, it is also one in which we can shower and bathe and attain a sense of redemption and renewal.

Bathrooms are private places where we isolate ourselves to prevent others from being offended, disgusted, or contaminated (what you will) and from seeing us naked and in our natural state. Bathrooms are also places where we undergo our private rituals of renewal. Body odors can be killed by perfumed products; minor afflictions can be remedied.

We retreat to the bathroom to renew ourselves and regain ourselves. (We also tend to judge other cultures by the nature of their bathrooms.) Thus some people find Italy and France "disgusting" because their bathrooms may not be as clean or modern as American ones . . . or Dutch or German ones. Indeed, there may be some kind of correlation between countries that are supremely mindful of their anuses and the poor quality of their food, and countries that are primarily concerned with the quality of their food and not terribly involved with their bathrooms and the softness of their toilet paper. America would be in the former camp, though there are many Americans who are trying to obtain the best of both worlds.

Our attitudes toward our bodies and natural functions, suggests Edward Dahlberg, are reflected in our literature. In *Can These Bones Live* he writes, "When you deny the male and female as they are, eating, sexually throbbing and giving off dense physical emanations, then you have the great STINK. Our misanthropy comes from one thing only, not man's poverty, politics, government, but the revulsion from his own ordure. As a result of this ablutionary ethic we produced a white and holy literature. But all holiness ends, as in *The Brothers Karamazov*, in the unspeakable stench of the corpse of Father Zosima" (1960, 66).

Dahlberg offers us an important insight into ourselves and our attitudes toward our bathrooms. Our literature, he believes, reflects our attitudes toward our bodies: We do not wish to confront the reality of bodily processes because ultimately we do not wish to confront the reality of our deaths. Thus we have created bathrooms that are designed to distract us from our bodies . . . we even have "designer bathrooms," with elegant toilets and water basins, and with fancy wallpaper, flowers or plants, plush rugs, and so on. Anything to distract us from the reality of body processes and body odors, which remind us of the stench of death.

Our bathrooms show how culture can shape our behavior. There are no "natural" attitudes toward the body, toward body processes, toward defecation and elimination, toward death. Our attitudes are always connected to cultural norms that, in turn, are generally connected to our social arrangements. Thus bathrooms can be signifiers of status, as in "executive" bathrooms that are reserved for important executives in corporations. A corner office (with light and a good view) and a bathroom reserved for oneself are two signs of status and power in America.

Little children often play with their feces and have to be taught to feel revulsion toward fecal matter. And if Freudian thinkers are correct, the toilet training of infants is a matter of profound importance, frequently traumatic for child and parents alike, which has a lasting impact on the psyche of the child. It is on the potty, our first bathroom, that we start being trained to function (in more ways than one) in society.

One of the most interesting developments in bathroom design is the "playpen shower pit" (as a real estate agent I know

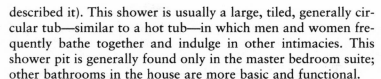

described it). This shower is usually a large, tiled, generally circular tub—similar to a hot tub—in which men and women frequently bathe together and indulge in other intimacies. This shower pit is generally found only in the master bedroom suite; other bathrooms in the house are more basic and functional.

Not that the bathroom is actually a functional room. For, curiously enough, studies have shown that bathroom fixtures are poorly designed and not built with utility in mind. The sink is usually too low for people, so they have to stoop over, and the toilet is not at the proper height for maximum comfort. But all of this is quite understandable, for when the unconscious emotions we have about our bodies and our wastes confront our sense of practicality, the vaunted American pragmatism flies out the window. Or should I say, to keep more directly to my subject, disappears down the drain.

ELEVEN

The Water Pik Shower

e-a- Berger

The Water Pik showerhead is not just another kind of shower-head that offers just another kind of shower. Water Piks try to emulate Jacuzzis and use water in pulsating spurts to exercise muscles and help generate good muscle tone. A shower is transformed into something more than a means of cleaning oneself, although this aspect of the experience is itself of considerable consequence.

We believe that water is connected to spiritual matters, a belief that may derive from the ritual of baptism. Water, we feel, some-how helps rid us of sin as well as related phenomena such as dirt.

But with the baptism (or its desacralized version, the bath), water is more passive. It dissolves things; it works slowly, perhaps even magically.

Mircea Eliade explains this relationship in his book *Patterns of Comparative Religion* when he writes, "In water everything is 'dissolved,' every 'form' is broken up, everything that has happened ceases to exist; nothing that was before remains after immersion in water. . . . Immersion is the equivalent, at the human level, of death at the cosmic level, of the cataclysm (the Flood) which periodically dissolves the world into the primeval ocean. Breaking up all forms, doing away with the past, water possesses this power of purifying, of regenerating, of giving new birth" (1958, 194).

The genius of the Water Pik is to take this purifying ability found in water and intensify it, put it under pressure and make it even more powerful. If in our view of things we have somehow learned to associate dirt (which, as Freud pointed out, is only matter in the wrong place) with sinfulness and corruption, then what better way of dealing with it than blasting it off our bodies with powerful streams of water?

There are trade-offs to be considered when we compare the shower and the bath. The bath more closely approximates the baptismal experience in that there is an immersion in water. There is also the pleasure of a regression to our prenatal state, when we were surrounded by amniotic fluid and lived in a condition of purity, an approximation of paradise. By contrast, the bathwater gets dirty, and as we soak in it we are reminded of our "sinfulness" and corruption. When we get out of the bath, we cannot escape a film of scum from this water, so that in a sense a bath is self-defeating. In addition, the ring around the bathtub serves to remind us of the fact of our dirtiness. Even if one is secular, this ring of dirt is unpleasant, a signifier of how dirty we were and will be again.

How much better it is, then, to take a shower, especially one with a Water Pik, and blast the dirt off our bodies and wash it down the drain. We may not get the psychological gratification of the immersion, but, instead, we get the feeling of supercleanliness and escape the reminder of our previous state.

In addition, we get the benefit of exercise without effort. Technology has provided a means of our cleaning ourselves and exercising our bodies at the same time and with no work on our part. There is something remarkable here: We do nothing (except turn on the water and stand under the shower), and we emerge fully exercised. Or perhaps, to be more accurate, massaged. We have replaced the masseur with a showerhead.

Somehow, with this kind of shower, force leads to ease, power leads to relaxation—just the opposite of what we might expect. This may be because there are two kinds of pressure we experience: psychological, or internal, pressure (which generates anxiety and fatigue), and physical, or external, pressure (which generates, under the right conditions, relaxation and a sense of well-being). Physical exertion and pain yield pleasure and that health of body that is necessary (so we are told) for the healthy mind.

There may also be a masochistic element in the Water Pik. After all, a pick is a pointed instrument used to penetrate and break up things (as in ice pick or dirt pick). The name "Water Pik" is meant to suggest a shower that shoots jets of water that are like picks, except that they don't penetrate the skin the way real picks do. Instead, they function like pinpricks and stimulate the flow of blood as they massage the body. Here we are back to the Puritans and the notion tied to them (perhaps falsely) that things that are unpleasant are good for you. There may be an element of pain connected with being "picked" by a powerful shower, but this pain leads, we are led to believe, to a higher physical and moral stage.

Once again we find that there is a sacred or spiritual dimension to a technological device—one that we may not be aware of but that we may sense in our subconscious. The feeling of well-being we get from a shower, our sense of bliss, which is magnified and intensified by the Water Pik, is connected to both physical and psychological matters.

In the Book of Genesis we read, "Dust thou art, and unto dust shalt thou return." We know this is true but feel that if we can take enough showers and wash the dust (dirt) down the drain, we can both keep this realization from our consciousness and, perhaps, postpone our returning to the dust for a bit longer. Water, Eliade has suggested, "nullifies the past" and provides a sense of renewal and rebirth. The Water Pik not only nullifies this past but blasts it to smithereens. It may not be the "fountain of life" that exists, we are told, in some magical place, but it is as close an approximation of it—psychologically, if not physically—as we can find.

T W E L V E

Bath Soap

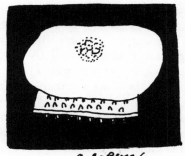

a-e-Berger

"Cleanliness," we say in America, "is next to godliness," which suggests that soap has a rather important role in the scheme of things. It functions, logic tells us, as an agent of the sacred. It is soap that enables us to redeem ourselves, to move from a state of being dirty (and ungodly) to one of being clean.

Bath soap can be seen, then, as a sacrificial agent. It gives of itself, it becomes diminished as we use it to clean ourselves. Like so many things in life, we don't actually see it dissolving, but we do notice, after using it for a week or so, that it is smaller. And we are older. Our days slip away and we notice very little change from day to day until we look at our soap bars.

At first our soap bars are substantial and solid . . . immune, it would seem, from the ravages of time and use. And then we notice, before we've used them that much, or so it seems, the soap bar has become thin and is about to break in two. It is merely a shadow of its former self, though we often continue to use it, carefully, as long as we can.

Soap dissolves from use, but it also has a tendency to self-destruct. One of the unsolved problems of modern society is how to keep soap from staying wet and dissolving. For if left in a little bit of water, soap becomes moist and slimy and dissolves. Soap must be kept dry in order for it to maintain its identity. When not being used for cleaning purposes, water is soap's enemy and air is its salvation. Soap thus finds itself in an ambiguous situation. Soap is an agent that uses water to fight against dirt. But the same water that soap needs to vanquish dirt is also a danger to it. From this we learn a moral: Things must be kept in their places. Soap must be protected from its friends.

Foam is a sign of soap's power, of its magic. Foam signifies luxury, softness, and ultimately, magic. How do these soft, insubstantial bubbles vanquish dirt and grime? we ask ourselves. In the Introduction I quoted Roland Barthes on the significance of foam and his notion that it signifies luxury and power in that huge volumes of it can be generated.

In other words, although soap may seem inert and relatively bland, it is in reality a very powerful and active entity. For it has the ability to produce foam. Soap can, somehow, spill out of itself enormous volumes of foam. We are close here to the miraculous—something out of nothing, a sudden intervention of a power that seems terribly insubstantial but is in reality of great force.

If this were all there was to bath soap it would still be an incredible object. But there is more to the subject, for soap has also been transmogrified from an agent of cleanliness to one of beauty. (There may be an association in our minds between cleanliness and beauty, but the connection is neither obvious nor immediate.) Bath soap now takes on a different significance. It facilitates beauty and thus has sexual implications.

And the soap bar itself has been turned into an artifact of beauty. Soap bars now come in all kinds of colors and shapes. Some bath soaps are even translucent, which suggests they are even more miraculous, for one can see "through" these soaps and not find anything in them that might be generating that wonderful foam. These soaps also have fragrances—of plants, flowers, and herbs, signifying their naturalness and identification with the luxurious. When one buys a bar of bath soap, one also obtains an identity, taken from the personality of the soap—as reflected in advertisements for it. Beauty, we learn, is our natural state. This beauty becomes masked by dirt, sweat, and other pollutants. What bath soap does is to return us to our original state, when we were naturally beautiful. Soap, then, is an agent of redemption that returns us to the Garden of Eden, if only momentarily, where our skin was clean and radiant.

Because we live in a modern industrialized society full of dirt and soot, we must be on continual guard and must wage constant battle with dirt. Thus we must, if we wish to be beautiful, keep using these soaps, for they alone have the power to redeem our beauty, to restore us to our original state of grace and loveliness.

We have all been taught that beauty is not just "skin deep" and that there are other, more profound, aspects to being beautiful. But the users of the various bath soaps believe that if beauty isn't skin deep, it at least starts at the skin. And a good start, as the saying goes, is half the battle.

THIRTEEN

Shampoos

The basic function of shampoo is to clean hair, but shampoos are much more complicated than that. Perhaps this is because our hair (and I'm thinking of the hair on the top of our heads, not body hair) is so important to us, psychologically speaking. Our hair is one of the few aspects of our bodies that we can manipulate with relative ease. With that freedom comes, all too frequently, the concomitant agony of choice.

One of the essential attributes of hair is that it can move, can take on a kind of "life" of its own, especially the long silky hair that some women have. This movement has a sexual allure, which probably lends the owner a heightened sexuality, a kind of glamour. This "life" that long hair has may be an indicator of the "life" that the longhaired woman is capable of generating.

We see this movement of hair exaggerated in shampoo commercials on television in which lovely young women bound across fields, their hair flying—almost undulating—in the wind. Long, silky, lively hair becomes connected in these commercials with natural beauty and perhaps with youthfulness. Long hair here signifies vitality, freedom, and lack of restraint.

Television commercials used to portray this concept by showing businesswomen with their hair pulled back and tightly controlled (and perhaps wearing big glasses) transforming themselves after work into "glamour girls." Off came the glasses, revealing stunning features. And down came the hair, flowing, streaming, undulating . . . reflecting the notion that now this woman is ready for love, romance, sexual pleasure.

For those not blessed with silky hair there are products that can be used to shape hair, to give it various "looks" that are meant to reflect the character of the wearer and her/his sense of style. This sense of style is heightened by the "personality" that advertising gives various shampoos. Shampoos are cosmetics, and when one uses a particular brand of shampoo, one is partaking of the personality of that shampoo and the sense of style and self it is meant to engender.

Hair, we are told, has "body," and this body must be kept in good "condition," so conditioner is, the ads would suggest, the moral equivalent of exercise. We shampoo our hair to clean it, to liberate it from its mortal enemy, the "greasies," and then we use conditioner to restore it to its allegedly natural goodness.

There is, then, a morality play involved with every shower and shampoo. For our own bodies are the very source of the pollution that we must fight with shampoo. For the most part, *we* generate this "grease" that shampoo must deal with. Our hair is the battleground between a "disgusting" secretion from our bodies that attempts to dull and pollute our hair, and shampoos, which rescue us from this debasement. The "greasies," then, are signs of the evil and ugliness in the human body, of our guilt, of that which contaminates from within. And shampoo now becomes an instrument of what might be called our cosmetic religions, which promise us salvation, which rescue us from natural sin and related matters.

This "religious" aspect of shampooing may explain why young people are so scrupulous about shampooing and why so many of them shampoo their hair every day. I see this kind of behavior as ritualistic, and where we find ritual, we generally find a belief system that can be defined as religious. If we can't be perfect, at least we can have perfect hair.

The "greasies" are a sign of the devil in this cosmology—or is it cosmetology? I would not suggest that the young people (and perhaps those not so young) who are caught up the way they are in ritualistic shampooing recognize this dimension of their behavior. All they know is that they want to have clean hair, which is necessary if they are to be popular and look good. But the imperatives behind this desire for perfect hair is, I would argue, a religious one.

Shampoo, then, liberates us from dirty hair (dirt here is a sign of pollution and sinfulness) and conditions our hair, which suggests that hair has a kind of life to it, perhaps even a body to hold that life. And shampoo also restores our hair. Here we are not too far from the realm of the magical or even the miraculous. Is it not conceivable, then, that the beauty we seek when we shampoo our hair is both physical and spiritual?

If this religious or sacred dimension to shampooing is true, then visits to hairdressers take on a different significance. We call these emporia "beauty parlors" or "beauty salons," but they can be looked upon as quasi-religious institutions devoted to more than just haircuts and shampoos. Hairdressers are not just artists but also—though it isn't obvious—priests and priestesses. Their function is only superficially to clean and cut our hair; on a deeper level it is to remake us, to help us be born again, via a ritual cleansing that signifies we are no longer impure, contaminated, or even our old selves.

This sacred dimension to shampooing is reflected also in the organic shampoos that are all "natural" and contain no detergents. We are returned, if only momentarily, to paradise, where, cleansed of corruption and pollution and smelling sweetly, we can live happily ever after. As long as our supply of organic shampoo lasts, that is.

Metonymy, not anatomy, is destiny!

FOURTEEN

Gel Toothpaste

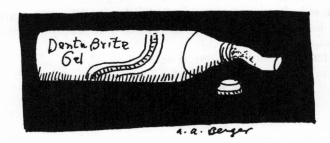

What is it about gel toothpaste that people like? What is its mystery? And why did the toothpaste manufacturers develop this product, anyway? It is hard to know for sure, but I think the appeal of gel toothpaste has something to do with the fact that it is essentially a combination of magic and science. The gel as it comes from the tube has a translucent color and a thick texture, unlike regular toothpaste, which is creamy and a bit softer. I think the color and the texture and translucent quality of the gel are important to people. The gel promises something different. And it hides nothing.

Technically a gel is a *colloid,* a combination of liquid and solid in suspension. As such, it seems to be a step forward from simple things like pastes, just as pastes were improvements on powders. But whereas a paste may be a useful modification of a powder, a gel is something entirely different, or so we are led to believe. What is fascinating about the gel is the way it slides out of the tube and, when we start brushing our teeth, turns magically into foam.

It is as if we liberate somehow the cleansing power that was held suspended in the gel when we start brushing our teeth. And it is as if some kind of magical transformation takes place as the gel turns, incredibly, into bubbles and the color disappears. This magical transmutation is an example of the kind of transformation that we believe we are all capable of achieving.

Like the gel, we are all, so we believe, combinations of capacities and limitations held, as it were, in "suspension." But ultimately we will free ourselves of our limitations and transform ourselves. Our gel toothpaste is a colloidal suspension that asks us to suspend our disbelief in magic (and ourselves). There is another aspect to gel toothpastes that might be worth considering, and that is the similarity between gel toothpastes and a popular dessert, Jello gelatin. Jello is a quintessential junk food made of gelatin, coloring, flavoring, and sugar. It may be that gels remind us, in various ways, of our childhood, when we liked Jello. Thus gels enable us to regress (in the service of our egos) to those "happy" days when love was unconditional.

Jello, which is full of sugar—in its traditional nonaspartame formulation—causes cavities, and gel toothpastes prevent cavities. Thus gels neutralize somehow (or so we would like to think) the sugar we took into our bodies when we were younger, more innocent, and less knowledgeable. Gels, in this respect, are kinds of "anti-Jello" substances, antidotes to past indulgences.

Gel toothpastes can be seen, then, as indicators of an unconscious belief on the part of those who use them in magic. They are signifiers of our belief that science ultimately is, though it may not seem to be, a realm involving magic. And magic, ultimately, is connected to power. (The notion that magic is a kind of thinking found in primitive societies and is prescientific must be cast aside here. Magic is a way of making sense of the world that exists along with what we call science and is found in modern societies—though often in camouflaged forms—as well as in allegedly preliterate ones.)

Just as a gel unites liquids and solids in a colloidal suspension, so do gel toothpastes unite science and magic. Gels may appeal to many people because they are the newest form of toothpaste, and we have a passion in America for the "newest," the "latest model," and that kind of thing. But underneath it all, when you get to the heart of the matter, the appeal of gel is to something very ancient.

Gels are "black magic" that promise white teeth.

FIFTEEN

Pajamas

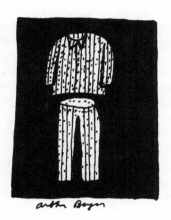

arth Bryn

Pajamas are an example of the extreme specialization one finds in modern societies. Different garments are available for different activities. The pajama, which originated in East India, is part of our sleepwear and is meant to mediate between our skins and bedsheets, which themselves are mediating objects.

Garments that are allowed to touch our skins have a special status, psychologically speaking. They must be soft and not irritate us, but they must also protect us from a variety of things, such as dirt, sweat, body fluids, and cold air. When we sleep we are vulnerable, so pajamas, which are our first line of protection, are probably more important psychologically than they are physically.

In their mediating position or status they are similar to the underwear we wear during the day, except that we change our underwear daily because it soaks up our sweat (and we do not wish to be defiled by our perspiration) but change our pajamas much less frequently because they don't get "dirty" as quickly.

Pajamas are similar in some respects to suits, except that pajamas are loose and comfortable while suits are more tight fitting and controlling. The pajama is a form of anti-suit suit meant for night wear, forming a barrier for us from sheets, comforters, and blankets. Interestingly, the pajama is not generally considered acceptable, on adults that is, even in family situations. That is one reason we have bathrobes. There is an element of shame at work here, and this has public as well as personal aspects. We are ashamed of our bodies, of the fact that our pajamas might smell a bit from sweat and other excretia, and so we protect ourselves from anxiety and others from embarrassment by covering over our pajamas with bathrobes.

The pajama is the most immediate "witness" to our sexual activities. Unless we make love in the nude, which is not too common, as studies suggest, the pajama is a silent participant. The pajama bottom thus may display signs of our sexual activities: perhaps some blood, perhaps some stains from semen. Thus we must cover up our pajamas with bathrobes to guard against the anxiety of revealing to others that we have been sexually active, especially in the family context in which there are small and perhaps inquisitive children.

On a more general level pajamas reflect our sense that we are "fallen" creatures. Why don't we sleep in the nude under our warm electric blankets or down comforters? Because nudity recalls the paradisiacal state in the Garden of Eden before Adam tasted of the tree of knowledge. Except for small groups of people who are nudists and who psychologically are trying to return to Eden, most of us feel uncomfortable when we are naked—except, that is, when we are showering or bathing and "rebaptising" ourselves. Even when it is very hot we do not usually sleep without clothes.

In *Ways of Seeing,* John Berger distinguishes between being naked and being nude. His discussion stems from his analysis of oil paintings of nude women who are "displayed" for men, but now that men are also being "displayed" for women, what he says applies to both sexes: "To be naked is to be oneself. To be nude is to be seen naked by others and yet not recognized for oneself. A naked body has to be seen as an object in order to become a nude. (The sight of it as an object stimulates the use of it as an object.) Nakedness reveals itself. Nudity is placed on display" (1972, 54).

Our wearing of pajamas suggests that we are troubled about being turned into objects of sexual desire and about admitting that we have sexual desires and appetites of our own. Also, when we are naked, Berger adds, "we are without disguise," a situation that we find intolerable.

So pajamas are involved with all kinds of anxieties and fears we have and play an important role in "covering us over" and protecting us from revealing our true selves—to our spouses and children and perhaps, even, to ourselves. Recall what Adam said to God in the Garden when God asked Adam where he was: "I heard thy voice in the garden and I was afraid because I was naked: and I hid myself."

When we want to hide, one way to do so is by putting on pajamas.

Broadloom Carpets

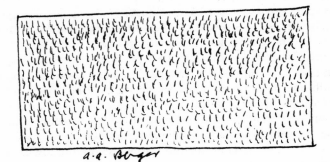

a.a. Berger

The essence of the broadloom carpet is completeness. The broadloom carpet strives for total coverage of floor space, for complete domination. It is possible to use broadloom carpeting as a rug and not have it wall-to-wall, but that really defeats the genius of the broadloom. Nowadays, with the cost of oak flooring as high as it is, builders tack down plywood flooring, for they know the houses will be covered from wall to wall with broadloom carpeting. This carpeting signifies "luxury" for the middle classes, who now never more have to worry about waxing oak floors or finding "area" rugs.

Real luxury, of course, is reserved for the truly affluent, who can afford handmade Oriental rugs. It is not uncommon, as a matter of fact, to find people putting Oriental rugs on top of their broadlooms. Once, rugs were reserved for royalty and captains of finance. The broadloom carpet changed all that, for now even the most humble workers can carpet their houses with broadloom. Thus there is a double imperative in the broadloom. Not only does it seek total domination of a floor space but it also strives for a kind of universal adoption . . . seeking acceptance from all classes.

And what do these carpets offer us? Why do we like broadloom carpets? For one thing, they help unify a room. Generally, broadloom carpeting does not have designs or varying colors in it, so it does add an element of simplicity to a room and, from a design standpoint, helps pull it together. In addition, it is soft to the foot and cushions one from the "hard reality" of, say, oak floors. (Or the harsher realities of plywood floors.) A fine broadloom rug is thick and, when laid over a good-quality rubber cushion, is soft and has a kind of luxurious aspect to it. It also is reputed to help conserve energy and cut down on noise by soaking it up. One feels, somehow, protected.

The very softness of the rug presents us with a dilemma. We want our broadloom carpeting to feel soft but we also want it to be "tough," to be long wearing. How do we combine softness and toughness, which seem to be antithetical? The answer is in the "miracle" fibers different companies have developed. These fibers often have, as someone suggested, names like Greek gods: Herculon (where the link is very obvious), Anso, Trevira, and so on. And these fibers have undergone rapid evolution, so that one can have a broadloom carpet woven from Anso IV, a fourth-generation fiber, no less.

These fibers, we are told, are tough and generally have special dirt-repelling abilities. And the carpets made from these fibers are tough and long-wearing as well as static-free. From the broadloom carpet we rediscover, then, something quite interesting, something we are always being told but that we never pay much attention to: In unity there is strength. There may be a political message in the broadloom carpet other than the most obvious one, that is, of embourgeoisement.

Easy access to broadloom carpeting convinces the masses (the embourgeoisement theory suggests) that they are middle class or bourgeois. There need not be a revolution since, as universal broadloom carpeting demonstrates, everyone has already achieved a middle-class status. We live, then, in a classless (because we are all middle-class) society. Broadloom carpet not only unifies a room or house, it unifies a nation.

There is also a paradisiacal aspect to the broadloom carpet that might be expected, given our history of utopian communities and our continual striving to escape from history (which we define as a record of domination, degradation, and defilement). The carpet is a mass-manufactured version, from this perspective, of the grassy paradisiacal state that existed in Eden before the Fall. With a broadloom carpet we return, psychologically, to the paradise that was ours in our earliest days.

Recall, for example, Andrew Marvell's lines in "The Garden." He writes, in one of the verses, "stumbling on melons as I pass/ensnared by flowers I fall on grass." In the middle-class paradises that we inhabit, when we fall, we will fall on a modern imitation of that primal grass, namely our broadloom carpets.

The broadloom carpet represents, then, an attempt to regain, in one sense at least (to the extent we can), paradise. We were expelled from Eden for tasting of the fruit of knowledge. We hope that as the result of one of the fruits of our new knowledge, especially chemistry, we can create the miracle fibers that will help us get back in. Or at least approximate the perfection of Eden as best we can. When you can create miracles by the yard, almost anything is possible.

SEVENTEEN

Slippers

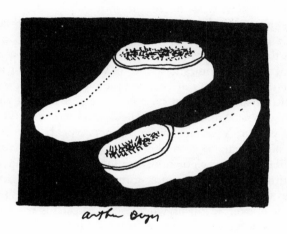

The essence of slippers is to be comfortable and soft. Slippers are meant, as their name implies, to be "slipped into" easily. They are worn around the house when one is relaxed and at ease. Slippers, then, contrast with shoes, which we associate with the outside world, the world of work and struggle. Shoes are generally made of leather, have shoelaces that are used to tighten the shoe around the foot, and have arches, so one can walk without getting tired. (The loafer, which is a shoe that does not have laces and is a "sport" or casual shoe, mediates between the slipper and the shoe. Loafers are shoes, but they have elements of slippers in them. Loafers are leather, have some kind of arch support, but can be slipped into.)

If you think about it, we must "work" to put on ordinary shoes. That is, we must tie shoelaces and, in some cases, squeeze our feet into the shoe with a shoehorn. There is an element of force and pressure here, of constriction. The foot is bound and perhaps even somewhat uncomfortable.

The existence of the slipper implies a classification system and ordering of experience. In this system there are two opposite realms: the world of work in which one wears shoes, and the world of rest, the domestic world, in which one wears slippers. And we signify that we are leaving the world of work when we take off our shoes and put on our slippers. When we wear our slippers we know that we can "relax" and forget about our jobs and the pressures we face in the business world.

The slipper can be seen as a kind of reward we give to our feet, a liberation from constraint and pressure. And slippers are, interestingly enough, common gifts for men. The tight-fitting business shoe, which puts pressure on the foot, reflects the pressure that is exerted on us when we work. Thus the slipper is meant to symbolize the escape from pressure, the release from "bondage" we feel when we take off our shoes (which also may be smelly from the perspiration we generated while wearing them) and slip into slippers.

When a woman gives a pair of slippers to a male there is a subliminal sexual significance to the act that must not be overlooked. The foot is a highly erotic part of the human body, although we are not always conscious of this significance.

As William A. Rossi writes in *The Sex Life of the Foot and Shoe*, the foot is "one of the body's most sensitive tactile organs, possessing its own 'sexual nerves'—and capable of the most intimate sensations in touching and being touched" (1976, 4). He adds, "The foot possesses and expresses the strange power of 'podolinguistics' or foot language—an innate ability to communicate feelings, attitudes, desires, especially as sexual and psychosexual symbols" (1976, 5). Rossi's book makes interesting reading, with fascinating discussions of the Chinese "podosexual" mania and all the tacky and kinky aspects connected with foot binding as well as other aspects of the foot as a sexual organ.

If shoes, consciously and subconsciously, convey psychosexual messages, what is the message of the slipper? Rossi makes it easy for us to figure this out when he writes, "The sexual kinship of the foot and shoe has been inevitable. While the foot has always been a phallic symbol, the shoe has always been a *yoni,* or vulva, symbol. This male (foot) and female (shoe) relationship is both ancient and universal" (1976, 13).

A woman who gives a pair of slippers to a man is giving a vulva or symbolic vagina that is easy to slip into, that is ready and accessible. Of course, this message is highly camouflaged and the woman giving the slippers is not aware, consciously, of the real message of the gift; the male does not realize it either.

Freud was to the point here. He comments, "The foot is a very primitive sexual symbol. . . . The shoe or slipper is, accordingly, often a symbol of the female genitals." And that is why slippers are gifts that entail more than we might imagine. Slippers are unconscious love offerings to men. Putting on a pair of slippers can be seen as a kind of symbolic rehearsal for the "real" thing that can be had later on.

From this perspective, we wear slippers when we get up in the morning to remind us (unconsciously, no doubt) of the sex we had the night before and we wear them when we come home from work to anticipate (unconsciously as well) the sex we hope to have. That explains why we feel so strongly about a good pair of slippers that we've gotten used to and are really comfortable.

Sometimes, putting on a pair of slippers is as far as a person gets or wants to go, sexually speaking. This may have something to do with the fact that we now tend to see sexual rela-

tions as a kind of work in which men must "perform": They must find "G-spots" and generate multiple orgasms. Various instruction books on sex, which resemble technical manuals, reflect this work orientation toward sex. Thus, if a man comes home from a hard day at work and doesn't wish to put on his slippers, there is a message being communicated, even though neither the man nor his wife are aware of what the message is or understand what is going on. Or might *not* be going on later that night.

E I G H T E E N

Electric Hair Dryers

The electric hair dryer, a relatively simple object consisting of a heating element and a small fan, is a great liberator. It enables us to dry our hair whenever we please after we've shampooed it, and quickly as well. We are no longer dependent on the sun to dry our hair, nor need we be forced to wait around for our hair to dry on days that aren't hot and sunny.

Shampooing is now possible in all weather, and we can benefit from the gratifications derived from shampooing more or less at our convenience. And since electric hair dryers are small, we can take them with us to the health club or when we travel.

One thing the electric hair dryer does is bring the beauty parlor into the house. This is in keeping with an imperative operating in contemporary American culture—to "institutionalize" the home, to bring into it devices and objects generally found in business establishments so that the home becomes a center of all kinds of activities that used to be conducted elsewhere. With the electric hair dryer we are all amateur hairstylists, and our houses are, among other things, beauty salons.

It is not possible to neglect the obviously phallic design of the typical portable electric hair dryer. A large number of them have pistol grips and look like guns, except that they are guns that generate hot air and do not fire bullets. These dryers permit us to dry our shampooed hair, which, we believe, will make us more attractive to the opposite sex or, in some cases, the same sex. Our beliefs about the power of our hair to glamourize us and make us desirable are reflected in every shampoo commercial.

Holding, using, and controlling a mechanical phallus cannot help but support our subconscious beliefs about our hair's sexual powers and potency. One rehearses with the hair dryer for what one hopes will be "the real thing" later on.

Doctrinaire Freudians (according to some thinkers, there are no other kinds) might even argue that using these hair dryers might be a way for women to assuage their "penis envy" and deal with the trauma of not having been born with the male's sexual apparatus. This leads in women, so the theory goes, to shame, a sense of deprivation and a rage against the mother for having been allowed to be born without a penis.

Interestingly enough, the nonportable electric dryers are womblike devices and are congruent with Erik Erikson's suggestion that women are "incorporative" and men are "penetrative." One might hypothesize that the large nonportable electric dryer, which is similar to the kind one finds in beauty parlors, would be popular with more traditional women who more or less accept the conventionally defined role of women in society.

The pistol/phallic type of hair dryer, in contrast, would be popular with more modern, assertive women. Psychoanalytically speaking, these women have gained control of phalluses (thereby generating castration anxiety in men) and feel very powerful. And for good reason, for they have both triumphed over their envy and generated deep-seated fears in men. (We cannot forget that in ancient Greek mythology, Medusa, with her hair of snakes, turned men into stone when they looked at her. Many women, it might be suggested, have a "Medusa Complex" and believe their hair, when shampooed and at its best, has the power to "knock men dead," so to speak.)

All of this, of course, like so much in our lives, goes on at the unconscious level. At the purely functional level an electric hair dryer is merely a simple device that generates hot air that dries wet hair. It is a convenience. But the shape of these devices and their connection with our hair, which we feel has a kind of sexual allure and power of its own, suggests that the hair dryer is much more than merely functional. The hair dryer may not reach to the roots of our hair, but it is intimately involved, I would suggest, with the roots of our being.

N I N E T E E N

Electric Toothbrushes

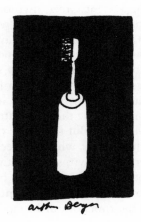

Why, of all things, an electric toothbrush? It seems at first sight to be one more preposterous object for the never-to-be-satisfied American gadget lover. It is that, of course, but it is more than that.

It was created, no doubt as so many gadgets are, because market research showed that it would sell. There are always, we must remember, very immediate economic reasons behind the objects that our industries make available to us. That is, there is money to be made. And there is, our society keeps telling us, nothing wrong with making money, generally speaking. *How* one makes money is a different matter.

The question we face when considering the electric toothbrush is this: Did people want electric toothbrushes or were people made to feel they wanted them? Was a need created somehow through clever advertising? To what degree, we might ask, can people be made to feel they want all kinds of things, some of which may not even exist as I write these words?

The genius of the electric toothbrush is that it turns everyone into a dentist. (And this process has been carried forward with the development of other dental gadgets that turn us into dental technicians.) Electric toothbrushes are parodies of the drills dentists use. But what's nice about these toothbrushes is that they generate no pain. And we come away from the experience of brushing our teeth with the feeling of exhilaration we get when we are released from the dentist's chair. No more anxiety, no more fear, no more sweaty palms or tenseness from the anticipation of pain.

Each time we brush our teeth with an electric toothbrush, then, we relive and triumph over the experience of going to the dentist and coming away with no cavities. And we hope that by attending to our teeth we can escape from the real dentist as easily as we escape from ourselves when we play dentist.

The amount of physical exertion used in brushing one's teeth by hand is quite minimal—there's no denying that. But brushing teeth is also terribly boring, and so we have created what is in reality a kind of handheld robot to do the job for us. An electric toothbrush should be looked upon, then, not so much as a toothbrush but as a robot that we have invented to do routine and mechanical tasks for us. It may even be that we do a better job of brushing teeth with the electric toothbrush than we do when we brush by hand. The electric motor doesn't know what boredom means, whereas we get bored very quickly when we brush our teeth by hand and generally want to get the task over with as soon as we can.

There is an element of anxiety we face when we encounter our mouths. For the mouth, more than any other area of the body, is one in which we must deal directly and continuously with decay and body fluids (saliva). This occasions anxiety and vague and fugitive feelings of disgust. After all, if you have to clean your teeth, that must mean that they are dirty. And dirt bothers us, especially when we feel that our bodies are dirty or in some way contaminated or diseased. There are odors that come from the mouth that trouble us. We know that particles of food become caught between our teeth and are attacked by bacteria. And there is the seemingly inexorable growth of plaque.

Given all this, what can be more reassuring than attacking our dirty mouths—and our dirty teeth, in particular—with what might be described as a form of "medical technology"? The electric toothbrush, from this point of view, represents "science," which, we all believe, will save us.

For young children, the electric toothbrush is one of the first objects they use that enables them to feel a sense of power, to control an electric gadget. The toothbrush is one of the first in a long line of gadgets and devices they will be using that cater to their command imperatives. It initiates them into the modern world.

Statistics show that Americans are having fewer and fewer cavities over time, but this is more a result of our fluoridated water than anything else. And so dentists must find different things to do for us. There are, in fact, too many dentists now, and many of the younger ones are having trouble making a decent living. Psychologically speaking, of course, there are always too many dentists. One dentist is too many dentists!

Ultimately, the electric toothbrush is a device that has utopian implications. For we would like to think that when we all have electric toothbrushes (and other devices for our teeth and gums) and can function, in a sense, as our own dentists, real dentists will no longer be necessary. A world without dentists, one in which they are no longer needed, may be as close as we can come to a definition of paradise.

T W E N T Y

Razors

$\textbf{S}$having presents the American male with a tragic dilemma: He must choose between competing ways of removing his facial hair, each of which is good in certain ways and bad in others. Thus, deciding upon what kind of technology you are going to use—razors with blades or electric shavers—becomes almost a moral choice. The way one shaves is a signifier or indicator of all kinds of hidden aspects of one's personality as well as a statement about one's stance toward matters such as the modern world, technology, and love.

The razor blade, in its various manifestations, makes its stand on its sharpness and the allegation that with a razor blade you get a "close" shave. It affords us the opportunity to use and control a sharp cutting instrument, appealing, then, to the old cavalier ethos. Shaving with a razor is a modern manifestation of swordplay, except that you use your sword on yourself and you do not use it to jab but to slice. The invention of the modern safety razor masks the danger in shaving with a sharp instrument, though it preserves a bit of the feeling of exhilaration men get when they have a lethal instrument in hand.

Our slang term for knife, "razor," preserves this aura of adventure and danger. People with "razors" (or, more precisely, some people with razors) are to be avoided if you value your life. The invention of the Trac II and Sensor razors concept by Gillette is a testimonial to our capacity to create gadgets of increasing complexity and to double consumption at the same time. A Trac II is like a double guillotine.

If these razors work the way they are supposed to, they represent a merciless attack on our facial hair. If you are going to be clean-cut, and we now have a choice in the matter with the recent popularity of beards in America, the Trac II and the Sensor (and razors by other companies as well) enable you to be so with a vengeance.

Shaving with a razor that uses blades is a sensual experience. We must not lose sight of this. You have the opportunity to spread hot lather on your face that you then shave off. The lather carries the stubble from your beard away, and by some wonderful process your face emerges clean and smooth from behind its mentholated (or scented) mask.

There is a kind of diffused sexual pleasure connected to shaving in this manner, in preparing oneself for the world this way. You even get a mildly masochistic "kick" from putting aftershave lotion on your raw skin. We might say that shaving with a razor blade and the various foams and ointments men use is a self-regarding (and, in a sense, perhaps even self-effacing) ritual. Aside from the physical pleasure men get in looking after themselves in this particularly sensual way, there are also fantasies of sexual conquest engendered by various advertisements and commercials for razors and aftershave lotions.

Very little of this physical and psychic gratification is available to the person who uses an electric razor. He is a person who doesn't want to bother with all the messy business connected with using a razor blade. He makes his stand on rationality, science, technology, and the machine. And he does not like the sight of blood—especially when it is his blood.

The companies that manufacture electric razors have developed a number of elegant, streamlined, supermodern designs for their products. This supports the men who use electric razors and confirms their prejudices regarding other kinds of shaving. Blades are considered to be anachronisms that modern and postmodern men must relinquish. The electric razor is pure functionality, the quintessence of logic. Its whirling blades "demolish" facial hair in a blitzkrieg attack.

You don't get quite as close a shave with an electric razor, but it's much faster, much cleaner (or less "messy" in any case), and infinitely more convenient. It is also, we have discovered, more dangerous in that our exposure to electric fields is very great when we use an electric razor. The so-called close shave one gets when one uses a razor with a blade must be seen as a prejudice one must cast aside in the name of modernity and functionality. And you can also use aftershave lotions.

In America, as in many other Western countries, shaving is a sign of manhood. And shaving is a ritual that signifies the transition from being a youth (or as it used to be put, "beardless youth") to being a "man." When we start shaving we cast aside our innocence and face a world of responsibility, complexity, conflict, and worry. One thing we must worry about is what kind of a razor we are going to use!

TWENTY-ONE

Underwear

a-a. Berger

Underwear has a decidedly inferior position and status in the scheme of things. It is defined by its relative position—under our clothes, where it mediates between our skin (nature) and our clothing (society, culture). But we do not call our suits and shirts outerwear or overwear, which would make sense if we were dealing with clothes in terms of their relative positions.

One might think that underwear is of no great concern to us, but that idea is a mistaken one. Underwear may be out of sight—though this is not always the case—but it certainly is not out of mind. The 1996 spring and summer J. C. Penney catalog devotes no fewer than six pages to underwear for men and additional pages to underwear for infants, children, young men, and women. What has happened is that underwear has moved from being an object defined in terms of its function to being an object of fashion and style.

Thus, one can be fashionable from the skin out. Underwear is no longer just something worn to soak up sweat and prevent our clothes from chafing. This movement from function to fashion is part of something socially significant: People have been turned into creatures vitally concerned about fashion in every aspect of their lives, another triumph for the advertising industry.

Underwear is no longer just white. T-shirts now come in many different colors, styles, and fabrics. One faces numerous dilemmas in choosing underwear—white or colors, all cotton or cotton and synthetic fabric, briefs or boxer-style shorts. There is great opportunity for choice here and for decisions about what one is really like. But why should garments that are not seen by others be "fashion" items? Why should we concern ourselves with being stylish when nobody will know the difference?

Part of the answer has to do with profits and merchandising. There is more money to be made on fashion items than regular ones (since there is no escaping fashion, one just downplays it with ordinary styles), so designers and retail stores are interested in developing fashion consciousness in consumers. There is also a tendency in fashion to be total, to absorb everything, to universalize itself. Once unleashed, fashion insists on making everything stylish. Designers are totalitarian, and fashion, more than we might imagine, is an ineluctable force that bends us to its wishes.

There are a number of forces at work here. We want to be loved, and looking attractive—if only in terms of our underwear—makes us, we feel (we *hope*), more worthy of love. We also feel that we deserve "the best," in our underwear as well as everything else. Thus, fashionable underwear is an indicator that we are "quality" people in every aspect of our being: underneath our skins and from the skin out. Having designer underwear shows that we are really first class, for we have good stuff even where people will never see it. (We deserve the best because we work hard. All luxuries are redefined as rewards for hard work.)

All of this is connected to a certain kind of narcissism, a sense of self-love that is manifested in trying to be attractive or desirable in as many areas as possible. We also find, with the development of underwear advertisements for men, that the male has been turned into an object of female lust (and perhaps male lust, in some cases). It is not unusual to see baseball players and other athletes wearing briefs in magazine advertisements. This so-called beefcake is a revolutionary development. Prior to it, only the female body was seen as a legitimate object of lust. Men would not allow themselves to be used that way.

The brief is important because it enables one to get a sense of the size of a man's genitals. Men are "judged" by the size of their "bulge," the male equivalent of women with large breasts. One thinks of dog shows or judging in cattle shows, for men are being evaluated in terms not of their good breeding but instead in terms of their breeding possibilities.

Underwear, then, has taken on a new role. Traditionally it existed to absorb sweat and protect one's outer garments. As such, underwear was an object of little concern, a sacrificial garment that existed to do dirty work, to absorb and free us from our sweat. It was humble and unassuming. Now underwear is something quite different. It has taken on airs, become stylish, been "designed" and turned into an object of fashion.

As this has occurred, men's psyches have changed. Men no longer are unconcerned with fashion, with style. And men's bodies are no longer able to escape from being objects of the

desire and lust of others. It used to be that men were judged in terms of social position, education, and manners. All of this has been stripped away, and men, like women, are now increasingly being judged in terms of their physical attributes. Perhaps men had it coming to them and deserve what they are getting.

Underwear, once magnificently plebeian and unassuming, once purely functional, has changed. Or been changed, to be more accurate. Men now can wear designer underwear, 100 percent nylon tricot coordinates if they wish, or briefs designed by the likes of Pierre Cardin. (President Clinton has revealed that he is bipartisan—he wears both boxers and briefs.)

One cannot help but wonder whether, in the matter of under-wear styles, change is a sign of progress.

TWENTY-TWO

Stockings

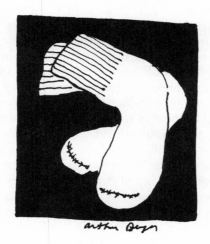

arthur Beyer

The stocking, more than any other article of clothing, bears the full weight of the human being. It is a mediating garment between the foot and the shoe and is given the task of protecting the foot from abuse. The essence of the stocking is toughness and endurance. Our stockings must be able to take all the physical stress that comes from continually being walked on, from being placed between the Scylla of the foot and the Charybdis of the shoe. In this position, stockings must be comfortable, absorbent, and durable.

If we do not wear stockings with shoes (and the idea of wearing shoes without stockings seems almost preposterous), we suffer from abrasion because our shoes rub directly against our feet, causing blisters and other discomforts. When we see someone wearing leather shoes without stockings we may assume that the person is either a bum or terribly absentminded. (Sandals are a different matter; they can be worn without stockings, though in general, proper people wear stockings with sandals.) Shoes imply stockings just as stockings imply shoes.

In addition to protecting the foot from abrasion, the stocking plays another role, one more social than physical. Stockings help contain the smells our feet generate. When we walk, the friction between our stockings and our shoes generates a great deal of heat. This heat in turn produces perspiration that cannot be dissipated because the shoe encloses the stocking and because leather "breathes" only to a limited degree.

Our feet, then, generally stink. And it is the stocking's fate to absorb this perspiration and contain foot odors. Stockings are like sponges in this respect. When we take off our shoes, especially if we've done a lot of walking, we become aware of the smells coming from our feet. That is why we like to take a shower, change our stockings, and put on a pair of slippers after a hard day's work. Body smells of any kind are generally distasteful to contemporary Americans, often generating (subconsciously) morbid thoughts and anxieties about death. Psychologically, the distance between smelly feet and putrefying corpses is not terribly great.

Complicating matters is the fact that the foot also is a sexual object. William A. Rossi, in his book *The Sex Life of the Foot and Shoe*, offers countless examples of the erotic elements of the foot, pointing out that the foot "has long played a direct role in sexual activity in foreplay and even in coitus. These practices are by no means limited to fetishists or offbeat sexual adventurers, but occur liberally among normal people the world over" (1976, 7).

If the foot has an erotic component to it and in fact often functions as a phallus, then stockings have a significance that becomes quite obvious. If their function is to mediate, to protect the foot, and to contain body excretions, is it not possible to see putting on a stocking as being similar to putting on a condom?

Our folklore makes this connection evident. Consider the following song boys learn:

> *In days of old,*
> *When knights were bold,*
> *And Frenchies weren't invented,*
> *They'd tie a sock*
> *Around their cock,*
> *And women were contented.*

This analogy becomes especially apt when one considers that an increasingly large percentage of men's stockings now come "stretch-to-fit" and fit tightly over our feet. It is probably best not to press too far this sexual aspect of putting on a pair of stockings. Yet there does seem to be a sexual component to stockings that must be taken into account.

And the fact that our feet smell and are subject to fungus infections such as athlete's foot suggests the kind of anxiety and ambivalence many men feel about sex. Women's genitals also smell (so we've learned from advertising), and we can get infections, or even die (due to AIDS), from sexual activity. Thus, our problems with our feet trigger in our psyches various ambiguous feelings and anxieties we have about sexuality.

Unlike prophylactics, however, we use our stockings over and over again. They are, to take a positive view of things, monuments to our ability to endure trauma, to suffer "martyrdom" and emerge triumphant, to be renewed and regenerated. Our stockings, if they are made of good stuff, "take it" and last—and so can we, we like to think.

Psychologists tell us that we follow a rather rigid order in putting on our clothes. Thus some people, without ever thinking about it, put on their left stocking first and others put on their right stocking first; they maintain this order of putting on their stockings (as well as their other clothes) throughout their lives. Orthodox Jews have no choice: They must put on their socks in a certain order. We develop private rituals that help us structure our lives and enable us to get through the day without having to devote thought to everything we do.

Instead of having to decide, each day, which foot we should put our stocking on first, we come to a decision (probably without being conscious of doing so) and are guided by it afterward. But where we find ritual, let me suggest, we find matters of considerable importance—regardless of how trivial the ritual might seem to be. Our stockings are, it turns out, intimately connected with attitudes and feelings we have (often hidden in our psyches) about death, disease, and sexuality. They may be inexpensive, but our stockings are not insignificant.

TWENTY-THREE

Shirts

For a long time shirts were signifiers of one's status in society. Sociologists divided people into "blue-collar" workers and "white-collar" workers and made numerous studies of the political beliefs and lifestyles of these two groupings. Blue-collar workers, so named because they wore blue chambray "work" shirts, were not as a rule well educated, did work that often required physical strength more than intellectual ability, and were seen as a kind of common man in America. Construction workers, carpenters, farmers, and laborers of all kinds were blue-collar workers.

Sociological studies of blue-collar workers indicated that they tended to be authoritarian, racist, sexist, and simplistic in their thinking ("dichotomous" was the term the social scientists used). In general, they were not the kind of noble types our founding fathers envisioned as populating America. White-collar workers, on the other hand, benefited from more education and, in turn, were shown to be (at least on the basis of the surveys) much more tolerant of others and, generally speaking, democratic. As one of the more popular textbooks on political science, *The Irony of Democracy* by Thomas Dye and L. Harmon Ziegler, put it a number of years ago: "It is the irony of democracy in America that elites, not masses, are most committed to democratic values. Despite a superficial commitment to the values of democracy, the American people have a surprisingly weak commitment to individual liberty, toleration of diversity, or freedom of expression for those who would challenge the existing order. . . . Democracy would not survive if it depended upon support for democratic values among the masses in America" (1975, 14). The authors cite a good deal of research that paints a fairly dismal picture of the "masses" (which we can interpret to mean essentially blue-collar types). The fact that these people vote less frequently, the authors suggest, is what enables our democracy to survive.

We know, of course, that not all blue-collar workers actually wear blue chambray work shirts, just as white-collar workers don't always wear white shirts. The white shirt has given way to the striped and patterned shirt. These two collars or colors are, of course, only meant to symbolize two elements in society. Nowadays everything is all mixed up, and you can't tell a person's occupation or status by the color of his or her collar.

Some social scientists have recently suggested that the old division between blue-collar and white-collar workers is no longer very useful. Many blue-collar workers earn more money than white-collar workers, though blue-collar workers still may not have the status that less-affluent white-collar workers have. It is better to describe jobs, many sociologists suggest, in terms of the amount of intelligence, creativity, and problem-solving they involve rather than in terms of the kind of shirt one wears to perform those jobs. Many blue-collar jobs are more interesting and challenging than white-collar jobs. A clerk in an office who does very routine work and is paid much less than a carpenter does not get more prestige than the carpenter. And it is prestige, perhaps a more accurate term than status, that is crucial here.

It may also be useful to consider how accurate the sociological studies of blue-collar workers are. There is always a chance that surveys obtain information that is not accurate or that they fail to capture the whole truth about their respondents. Since we are very complicated animals, it is hard to get reliable information about us on surveys and questionnaires.

Furthermore, as a result of economic developments, it is not unusual to find increasingly larger numbers of more highly educated people ending up in blue-collar jobs, especially those that are not routine or relatively simple. It may be, in fact, that many "white-collar" people are doing "blue-collar" jobs. The American dream involves people rising in the world, which used to mean moving from blue-collar jobs to white-collar ones. That may not be as easy as it once was, and if the sociologists are correct, it may not even be desirable. The sociologists who present blue-collar types as terrible are themselves white-collar workers who probably come from blue-collar families and in any case, ironically, often make less money than many blue-collar workers.

TWENTY-FOUR

Ties

Ties are signs of the white-collar worker, the professional, the person who works in what is now called the information society. So-called blue-collar workers do not, as a rule, wear ties with their denim shirts (though some blue-collar workers who wear company uniforms do wear ties with them, but uniforms are a different matter).

The word "tie" suggests some kind of a connection or link with something, and indeed, ties do have that function. On the most immediate level, they bind us. We "knot" ties around our necks, giving the tie a function as a kind of decorator noose, one might say.

Ties exert a kind of subtle pressure on us, which is why, when we want to relax or are in situations in which we no longer need to be as formal as we are when wearing ties, we loosen them. (This gesture often is accompanied by opening the top button of the shirt.) One is now in some kind of "action" mode in which social etiquette no longer is very important.

In such situations we are, so to speak, "untied." The tie, when worn, is a reminder of our status and role in the world. Ties connote seriousness, formality, perhaps even dignity. They also enable us to show our sense of style. One finds that styles in ties are connected with such things as age, profession, and status. Older businessmen tend to wear different kinds of ties than younger ones do, or than professors or intellectuals do. The pattern of the tie, the fabric, even the kind of knot used— all are signifiers of the person wearing it.

Consider the bow tie. A bow tie is a strong statement and is "read" by most people as such. People who wear bow ties are emphasizing that they are different from the ordinary person. Bow ties are associated with intellectuals, writers, and "creative" personalities. The bow-tie wearer agrees to go along with the convention that ties should be worn but refuses to wear the ordinary or conventional kind of tie.

Ties also can be used to advertise various affiliations one has. English schoolchildren, boys as well as girls, generally wear uniforms with their school colors, and an important part of that uniform is the school tie. One can tell at a glance what school a person is attending. That tie tells us a great deal about his or her social class and status. A tie from Eton, for example, suggests all kinds of things about the wearer—and his life chances.

Making children wear a shirt and tie also seems to have a kind of calming effect on them. A shirt and tie tend to give a youngster an image of himself or herself (in cases where girls wear uniforms with ties) as a part of adult society. The attire is more formal, more social, more restraining. A young boy in a white shirt, cap, school tie, school slacks, and black leather shoes—in a common British schoolboy's uniform, that is—behaves differently than he would if wearing a T-shirt, blue jeans, and sneakers, which is the "non-uniform" uniform of American schoolboys.

The tie itself constrains physically. But it is also a symbol of a society that treats children differently. When children wear ties in England, they are acknowledging that there is a social order that exists and to which, in various ways, they must accommodate themselves. American children do not learn this lesson. For American children, society is for the most part an abstraction. A kind of rude shock awaits them when they enter the business world, which has all kinds of conventions and rules (sometimes unwritten) about what kind of dress is proper—even, perhaps, about what kind of tie must be worn.

In recent years in America there has been an interesting development. Companies are now having "corporate ties" made for directors, clients, and other important people. These ties incorporate the business's colors or logo in order to identify the wearer with the company or one of its products.

An old *Time* magazine article on the subject (October 13, 1980), titled "A Rage for Ties That Bind: The Stylish Executive Now Wears a Company Cravat," tells us: "A time-honored British tradition—the old school tie—is now taking root in American business. In Britain, graduates of Oxbridge colleges, officers of army regiments and members of London clubs have long worn institutional ties as a way of recognizing other 'old boys' without asking. Now Americans can pick out a colleague or competitor at a sales convention according to the cravat around his neck. . . . Far from being crass advertisements for the wearer's employer, company chokers tend to be stylish, subtle, discreet." The article points out that fancy silk versions of these ties are reserved for the upper echelons of the corporations but that "more pedestrian polyester" versions are often offered to middle-level employees—at cost.

The development of the company tie is a logical extension of the function of the tie itself—to connect a person with society and to demonstrate that the person recognizes a social order. This is the function of ties in general. The school tie, the corporate tie, even the designer tie—with someone's initials or logo used in the design of the tie—all of these are mere extensions of the basic function of the tie. Ties enable people to tell others something about themselves, often something they consider important. Ties are also aesthetic objects. They are often made with beautiful fabrics, have handsome designs, and are, in addition to their utilitarian functions, works of art.

TWENTY-FIVE

Suits

A suit, technically speaking, is an outer garment with two (or sometimes three) pieces: a pair of pants, a coat, perhaps a vest. The essence of the suit lies in its uniformity. That is, the pieces all match and are made of the same fabric.

Suits occupy a particular position in our codes of dress. They are the most formal of our everyday wear and are at the opposite pole from leisure wear (though, interestingly enough, we used to talk about leisure suits). In between these two polarities we find the sport coat and slacks, which have a kind of ambiguous status.

The striped, vested three-piece suit has become something of a cliché in recent years—a signifier of solemnity, status, reserve, and power. We find lawyers, accountants, and businesspeople of certain kinds wearing this outfit now. It has become the official costume of people who work in the information society, of professional people who want to be taken seriously.

It has been argued that all male costuming is connected to work. As Johan Huizinga writes in *The Waning of the Middle Ages*, "The modern male costume since the end of the eighteenth century is essentially a workman's dress. Since political progress and social perfection have stood foremost in general appreciation, and the ideal itself is sought in the highest production and most equitable distribution of goods, there is no longer any need for playing the hero or the sage" (1924, 39). The suit, I would suggest, is more than anything else the epitome of professional business dress and reflects an important change in the modern psyche.

Work and the production of goods now is central to our being, and since this is the case, we wear clothes that facilitate work. Our clothes are a reflection of our values and preoccupations. All this is connected to our democratic value system and to an egalitarian belief system that is connected to our faith in democracy.

But work has not always been central to our lives, just as we have not always believed in democracy and equality. "In aristocratic periods, on the other hand," Huizinga tells us, "to be representative of true culture means to produce by conduct, by manners, by costume, by deportment, the illusion of a heroic being, full of dignity and honor, of wisdom and, at all events, of courtesy" (1924, 39).

How strange these terms sound to us, how infinitely far removed from our experience and even from our expectations.

Manners, deportment, dignity, honor, wisdom—these are all virtues that seem terribly anachronistic and only dimly a part of our memory.

Modern businesspeople in their business suits have a different perspective on things. Profits, promotions, and success are the goals in a cutthroat world where courtesy seems hopelessly old-fashioned and, worst of all, counterproductive.

The suit is the signifier of the antihero who lives in an age not conducive to heroism, or even the "illusion" of heroism. This may explain why, generally speaking, we garb the heroes of our fictions (films, comic strips, animation) in strange and often very colorful costumes: capes, cowboy hats, uniforms, and space suits. Superman is an interesting figure for us, for in him we find a hero camouflaged in a suit and a bumbling persona. Perhaps he stands as a paradigmatic hero for many businessmen who see themselves as, if not heroic, then at least capable of maintaining some kind of illusion about their heroism. The business suit is only a front they wear to function in the marketplace. When they are through with work, they change into a costume that is more congruent with the heroic vision, once they find the moral equivalent of a telephone booth.

This kind of behavior may be possible, but it imposes terrible strains on people, for they must attempt to maintain two distinct personalities, two separate philosophies, two opposing perspectives on things. We become split with two competing worldviews to balance—unless, that is, we can completely switch from one personality to another and are able to contain two separate identities.

But all this is only for those who maintain ambivalent feelings about the businessman. For most, the businessman in his striped three-piece business suit represents the ideal to which they aspire. In America, which never experienced feudalism and thus never had much experience with ideals of heroism, our "holy grail" is the mighty dollar.

Perhaps there's good reason to base our society and values on equality. In the Middle Ages, only a favored few were able to pursue the heroic ideal. For the rest, life was rather grim. But wouldn't it be wonderful if, somehow, we could figure out a way to combine the positive side of the heroic ideal with the idea of equality? For this would produce legitimate heroic figures who have manners and a sense of honor, as well as figures who wear pinstriped suits and who know how to get good results on the bottom line.

TWENTY-SIX

Shoes

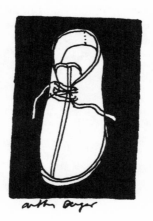

If stockings are condoms, what are shoes?

This question leads us right to the heart of the matter, forcing us to consider the erotic and sexual aspects of the foot and the things we wear on it. Generally speaking, the erotic aspects of our shoes are submerged in their functional and aesthetic elements and thus evade our consciousness. But just because we are not conscious or aware of something doesn't mean we aren't being affected by it.

The shoe is an incorporative article of clothing. Because of its erotic nature, the foot has a powerful sexual significance, and putting on a shoe can be seen as a metaphor for having sex as the masculine foot penetrates the feminine shoe. As William A. Rossi reminds us in *The Sex Life of the Foot and Shoe,* the "male (foot) and female (shoe) relationship is both ancient and universal" (1976, 13).

It is the submerged sexual aspects of the shoe that explain why purchasing shoes is a very difficult task for so many people. For a pair of shoes has a number of different functions—not merely protection or comfort. I've heard some people talking about having to "fall in love" with a pair of shoes before they buy them.

Shoes in themselves often have a strong aesthetic component. They can be beautiful objects in their own right; they can be made of fine leather, can show craftsmanship, have different designs, and so on. Thus, a pair of beautiful shoes enhances the person wearing them.

This aesthetic-sexual dimension of shoes can lead to fetishism in people. I once met a woman who loved shoes so much that she had purchased more than two hundred pairs of them. Some that she thought particularly beautiful didn't even fit her, as a matter of fact. She just wanted to own them as beautiful objects. And the case of Imelda Marcos and her three thousand pairs of shoes is well known also.

Not many people go this far, but many people do have quite a few pairs of shoes, showing that the same impulse is at play, though not in as severe a form. Shoes tell others a great deal about us.

The businessman generally wears rather conservative shoes with relatively thin leather soles. (Heavy shoes with thick soles are found in work shoes worn by blue-collar workers . . . and, in recent years, college students.) Usually business shoes have laces that are tied tightly. When relaxing, however, we wear "sporty" shoes that may be made of soft leathers with thick rubber soles. Some forms of these shoe are called, appropriately enough, "loafers."

And, of course, for every sport there are appropriate shoes: running shoes for joggers, tennis shoes for tennis players, hiking shoes for backpackers, and basketball shoes that often cost more than one hundred dollars a pair. Furthermore, shoes have become objects of style; thus we have changing fashions in shoes, which means we feel obliged to buy the latest "hot" style if we wish to be fashionable.

Fashion, we must remember, is a powerful social force that carries people along with it. There is a coercive aspect to fashion. If one wishes to remain relatively inconspicuous and not stand out or be different, one must change with the styles—one must constantly change to "stay the same" (that is, to remain inconspicuous). When fashion is introduced to men's shoes, or any aspect of men's clothing, there are economic gains to be made by the manufacturers of shoes and psychic (and perhaps even financial) penalties to be paid by the wearers of the wrong shoes.

Shoes no longer have the ability they once had to give us a social identity and to suggest our status, for some people from the working classes have taken to wearing shoes that are "above" them. And we have lost the sense of the permanence things had when we wore the same pair of shoes or style of shoes for long periods of time. An old, comfortable pair of shoes used to be one of the most immediate consolations we had in the world. Now fashion has stripped us of that—at least as far as the workplace is concerned.

I have not discussed women's shoes here. They have obvious sexual aspects: display, the tilting of the body when high heels are worn so as to emphasize the breasts and other sexual characteristics, forcing the woman to walk in a certain way. This sexual aspect of the shoe is reflected in the Cinderella story, where the prince discovers Cinderella by putting a glass slipper on her foot and getting a perfect fit.

We put on the shoe to venture out in the world. Both the shoes we wear and the act of putting them on are, we discover, loaded with sexual significance. Shoes tell us a great deal, though they say nothing.

Except, of course, when they squeak.

TWENTY-SEVEN

Kitchens

The kitchen is the room that builders use to sell houses to women. This is because women, even though they have been "liberated," still do most of the cooking in American families. So kitchens are designed to appeal to women—to be pleasant yet functional. As a builder once said to me, "The little woman spends a lot of time in the kitchen, so you want to make her as happy as you can."

Once, women *did* spend a great deal of time in kitchens, and some still do. But with the development of the two-income family, women don't have as much time to devote to cooking, though studies have shown that women who work still end up doing a major portion of their family's cooking and housework in addition to their regular jobs. Kitchens are the centers of family life, if only because they are the one place where the family gathers regularly. (I'm assuming we are talking about an "optimal" kitchen, which has room for people to sit down and eat.)

This means that kitchens end up as trauma centers, for it is at the family meals that a good deal of fighting and bickering that goes on in families takes place. Meals are frequently the occasion for family fights, for resentments to be aired, for complaints, for insults, and that kind of thing.

The kitchen is a power domain, and it is interesting to note that the average woman in her kitchen "commands" a number of powerful electrical or electromechanical devices: disposals, trash compactors, microwave ovens, can openers, blenders, food processors, bread machines, and liquifiers, among other things. Ironically, women have at their fingertips and generally use a number of powerful machines and devices whereas men, if they are typical and work in the information sector of our society, have little contact with powerful machines (with the exception of their automobiles and computers, that is).

In many respects the kitchen is like a nineteenth-century factory, with powerful machines used to "manufacture" various products: breakfast, lunch, and dinner. And the woman who labors in the kitchen is like a factory worker condemned to eternal servitude. There is no end to a woman's work in the kitchen. (The old saying "A man's work ends with the setting sun, but a woman's work is never done" is absolutely true.) Many men, of course, often bring home things to do for their jobs, so their work isn't necessarily done when they leave their offices. But there is no end to cooking and cleaning, and the rewards for doing them are meager at best.

Thus men have invented various devices to make things easier for their wives. This is so the hatred women feel for their husbands (for having trapped them into a life of unending Sisyphean domestic labor) can be, it is hoped, diminished. And the women get, at least, a sense of power along with a diffuse kind of sexual pleasure from commanding and controlling these devices.

Most of the devices found in the kitchen are, generally speaking, "incorporative," in keeping with the incorporative sexual modality of women. (The psychologist Erik Erikson, as I noted earlier, uses these terms. He has suggested, based to a degree on his observation of young boys and girls playing with blocks and building towers and chambers, that men are basically "penetrating" beings and women are "incorporative" ones. This, of course, parallels human sexual apparatuses.)

Refrigerators, dishwashers, ovens, trash compactors, food processors, microwaves, and electronic bread machines are all objects into which things can be put. There is, psychologically speaking, a perfectly symmetrical relationship here: Incorporative beings control incorporative devices. One of the few "male" devices found in the kitchen is the electric knife, but it is not a standard device and is generally used by men when they are carving turkeys and roasts.

With the development of computers and other electronic (as contrasted with electromechanical) devices, we now find sophisticated and extremely complicated versions of the old appliances, though most are still essentially mechanical. The only exception to this would be the microwave oven, which is a "high technology" device.

We see an element of cultural lag here. Women are still in the nineteenth century, for the most part, with relatively crude mechanical devices, whereas men have abandoned these devices as quickly as possible and gone electronic.

Where men must be involved with machines and the old technology, they now, to the extent they can, invent robots to do the "dirty work." But large numbers of women are still, it seems, able to be mesmerized by the appliances found in modern kitchens. Kitchens are not really "high tech" but, instead, imitation high tech, industrialized and mechanized with elements of the new technology used here and there.

The industrialization of our kitchens reflects how the family in America has been undergoing considerable modification. (Half the marriages end in divorce, and the number of one-parent families is growing.) Some years ago I wrote an essay, somewhat facetiously I must admit, in which I argued that we were undergoing a process I called "motelization." Parents were being reduced to the status of motel keepers, relegated to the task, essentially, of taking care of their children's laundry and preparing meals. Their children, with their own cars and own rooms, needed only their own entrances to their rooms in order to turn the average house into a "motel." In many respects that seems to have come true, except that these motels generally are now run by one person and are "mom" operations rather than two-person "mom and pop" operations.

The final irony, of course, is that the modern kitchen, full of labor-saving devices, powerful appliances that respond instantly to a light touch, is used less and less. Many Americans are too busy working, making enough money so they can lead the good life, to have time to cook and eat together the way families did in the old days. We eat more and more in fast-food restaurants. (Something like one out of every three meals is eaten out, and that figure is expected to jump to two out of every three meals in another decade or two.) And we've turned our kitchens into the moral equivalent of fast-food restaurants as well.

One of the signs that one is leading the good life nowadays is to have a large, up-to-date, gadget-filled, postmodern kitchen. And not use it!

TWENTY-EIGHT

The Refrigerator

Cold preserves food. This fact makes the refrigerator possible and this, in turn, makes modern society possible. For the refrigerator liberates us from daily shopping, which means supermarkets now make sense, because there one can purchase enough food for a week (or longer) and be freed from the daily chore of shopping.

The refrigerator has grown in size (as have our supermarkets) and now often has a huge capacity. Combined with a freezer, this device enables a family to store enormous quantities of food. A look at typical refrigerator advertisements in magazines suggests that the typical American family eats prodigious amounts of meat, vegetables, fruits, and dairy products.

There is a kind of paradisiacal element to the full refrigerator: It is psychologically reassuring to know that one has all that food on hand, that one will not go hungry. Ironically, we have these full refrigerators and at the same time we worry constantly about our eating and continually go on and off diets. Whatever hunger most of us feel as adults is self-induced.

And, I would imagine, the greater the amount of food on hand in the bulging refrigerator, the greater the sense of sacrifice on the part of the dieter. We like to think that we in modern society have transcended the mad passions of the Middle Ages, but how much difference is there between the religious fast and the beauty diet? Not too much, if you think about it.

Modern dieters resemble the religious zealots of the Middle Ages. Dieters are tormented continually by their inability to sustain their diets, by their "falling" from grace and not being able to control their animal appetites. We smile with incredulity when we hear of religious hermits who lived in caves and ate thorns, but how much different is this from a life of continual dieting or, in the most extreme forms, from anorexia?

I have suggested that there are economic reasons why our refrigerators are so large. One can have a minisupermarket in one's home and, thus liberated from daily shopping, be free to work. This applies in particular to women. They have been "liberated" from domestic chores and are free to work in the outside world. It turns out, studies show, that these liberated housewives end up doing a major percentage of the cooking and homemaking when they return from work, so their "liberation" ultimately frees them to work twice as hard as they previously did.

There are also psychological reasons for these large refrigerators. Is it not possible that many of the people who purchase big refrigerators, in addition to starving themselves continually on their diets, were also starved when they were babies? Certain guidebooks to raising children (popular years ago) suggested babies should not be fed on demand lest they become "spoiled," dominating, and uncontrolled. Thus some babies who happened to be hungry when it wasn't feeding time were not fed and knew, at an early age, intense hunger. In these cases we cannot blame the parents, who were only doing what they thought was right for the children. Nevertheless, these babies experienced starvation. They might have cried themselves to sleep in a rage.

Is it any wonder then that so many Americans have terrific anxieties about food? This may explain why we have such huge refrigerators and freezers and why so many Americans are overweight. The refrigerators and fat are means of coping with powerful anxieties we feel that are connected with starving. A study of prep schools made by a couple of sociologists found that one of the most traumatic things that happened to young men in these schools involved losing access to a full refrigerator—the moral equivalent, from our perspective, of being kicked out of paradise.

And dieting, from this perspective, may involve a kind of regression to childhood—when we did not have to perform, when we knew absolute love, and when we knew nothing about death—and when we experienced, in varying degrees, hunger and starvation.

This might also explain the various cryonic societies found in America. People who join these societies pay money to be frozen at the moment of their deaths in the hope that they can be awakened, in the future, when science and technology have discovered ways of dealing with the causes of their deaths (and perhaps death itself). Being frozen is a negative or reverse aspect of being in a womb—or returning to it; one is old instead of young and one is frozen instead of kept warm.

One of the final ironies relating to the refrigerator is that despite the paradisiacal abundance it offers, Americans are cooking less and less, and what they are cooking increasingly involves frozen foods that can be popped into microwave ovens and cooked in an instant. The promise the refrigerator holds out is not realized because all too frequently we are too busy working to have time to cook very much.

Thus the refrigerator with its freezer stands as a symbol of an unrealized paradisiacal state. There is food there, but some of it (for a variety of reasons) cannot be eaten. The larger the refrigerator, the greater the sacrifice, the more extreme the renunciation.

Hell, we are told, is hot. Perhaps—but I can envision it as full of bulging refrigerators and tormented souls who are on diets, or who are avoiding meat, or who don't like vegetables, for eternities.

TWENTY-NINE

Supermarkets

The supermarket is an omnipresent institution in American culture. Shopping in supermarkets, we must realize, is not just a random activity but is instead a highly structured ritualized one in which the customer is led, more or less unsuspectingly, along preselected pathways. The supermarket is a labyrinth through which we wander, and our movement in this maze is more preordained and directed than we think.

I also believe that supermarkets should be looked upon as media that "broadcast" food and related items. They use other media, the newspapers and television, to advertise, but they are themselves media in that they carry something and spread it to the public. We can look at supermarkets in terms of their structures and find the following oppositions in them: basic foods versus convenience foods, perishables versus staples, red meat versus green vegetables, a periphery and an interior, and most importantly, free entrance and payment on leaving. (This free entrance is now being challenged by giant stores such as Costco, which charge a yearly fee for membership.) The basic opposition is between merchandise and money, which is the key to obtaining the ten or fifteen thousand items in the typical supermarket.

The design of supermarkets is very interesting. I will use a supermarket near Mill Valley, California, as a typical example here to show what we find when we look at supermarkets in terms of their structure.

The front is always where we find the cashiers. Symbolically, the front of supermarkets is always black, since money is, psychologically speaking, "filthy lucre." At the rear we often find dairy products, which are white and symbolically clean. Milk and milk products are "innocent." On the right hand wall, as one faces the rear of the store, we find vegetables and fruit (green) and on the left hand wall we find meat and poultry (red). The oppositions in this particular store—the one I shop at—are black versus white (front to back) and red versus green (side to side).

All of these items are on the perimeter, where high-volume and high-profit items are sold. The inside of the store, known to the trade as "the jungle," is where we find staples. One of the basic problems for supermarket designers is luring people into the jungle and getting them to spend time there. Statistics reveal that there is a direct correlation between the amount of time we spend in a supermarket and the amount of money we spend.

The more time we spend, the more money we spend, so in supermarkets time really is money.

The problem shoppers face is how to navigate the supermarket so they pass all aisles and can get whatever it is they are looking for as quickly as possible. Generally, people adopt strategies for shopping and moving around in supermarkets. Some do the circumference first and then weave in and out of the aisles, and others do the aisles and cover the circumference as they go. Others have lists and only go to selected areas.

Most people when they enter a supermarket go to the right and start along the right hand wall, regardless of how the supermarket is laid out. There are different theories of supermarket design that put different kinds of products along this right hand-wall. In some markets we find meat, in others bread, in others cosmetics, and so on.

An examination of supermarkets is very revealing, for we find that, generally speaking, cultural priorities are reflected in the products sold. Thus, the enormous amount of space devoted to dog food and cat food tells us something about the place of pets in American society. (The pet food and products industry is a multibillion-dollar industry now.) The space devoted to frozen foods and instant foods also reveals something about our attitudes toward time and toward eating.

Within supermarkets people go into semihypnotic trances due to the "information overload" they undergo as their eyes (and senses in general) are attacked by the thousands of different products, all of which compete for attention via arrangement and packaging. Supermarkets are fantasy lands and generate dream states, paradisiacal in nature, in which one wanders through a land of milk and honey (literally) and fruits and beefsteaks and on and on. Connected to all of this are the numerous fantasies we've picked up from television commercials about many of these products.

There is, of course, a grim reckoning we must face after our forty minutes of wandering through this Muzak-filled mock paradise. For, ultimately, we must confront two monsters—the erratic checkout clerk (now aided by his or her scanner) and his electromechanical Cerberus, the cash register and various credit card devices we can use to pay for our purchases. They are surrounded by high-profit "impulse items," the last chance supermarket companies have to get us to buy things during a moment when we are extremely susceptible to the impulse to buy.

Every week, and sometimes more than once a week, we undergo this ritual, exchanging "dirty" money for clean food, surviving yet another ordeal in the labyrinth and facing the Minotaur. The Minotaur in the supermarket labyrinth is not lurking in the middle of it but at the exit, and he is always willing to spare us for the right ransom. For many people, surviving the supermarket ordeal and the encounter with the Minotaur/checkout clerk is as close as they ever get to heroism.

THIRTY

The Morning Newspaper

With the rise of television viewing, the evening newspapers in America's larger cities find themselves locked in a kind of death grip. They cannot compete with television, which shows people the news as it is happening, though, admittedly, television news is generally little more than a headline service. Often, because of traffic problems, the evening dailies have trouble even distributing their newspapers to suburban areas. (Ironically, evening newspapers in suburban areas, which are often little more than glorified shoppers, are prospering.)

146

Morning newspapers, however, are surviving and even doing rather well, though whether they can survive in their present form is not certain. They face competition from the radio, from television, and from new technologies that are being developed. The morning newspaper provides each day a mosaic of life, a picture of the shifting sands on which we must, somehow, secure a footing. Every morning there are hopes of pleasant surprises to be found in the paper as well as anxieties about unpleasant ones.

And so we fetch our morning paper with a combination of anticipation and dread. There are often surprises, but not too many of them are happy ones. Instead there is what seems to be an endless succession of tragedies, misfortunes, and accidents. We read the newspaper ultimately as a defensive measure—so we will not be caught unawares. That is probably the reason we watch the news on television the night before.

What we get in the morning newspaper is what I call a "ground," and we who read the papers are "figures" who make sense of the world and our lives against that ground. Because meaning is based in part on a relationship between figures and grounds, the morning paper helps us find meaning in life and develop a stronger sense of personal identity.

Human beings are naturally curious animals, and the morning newspaper helps us assuage this curiosity with a blend of political and economic news, sports, entertainment features, comics, trivia, and advertisements. Most people, so research indicates, tend to glance at the headlines, read a paragraph or two in a number of stories, and then move on to the so-called soft news (or entertainment) features of the paper. Here we find out about the amorous intrigues of movie stars, get information about sports, and find the comic pages.

News, as Marshall McLuhan explains things, is always bad news. Good news is advertising. In the newspaper we start with the bad news on the front page and in the front section of the paper and then move on toward the entertainment sections, so we can look upon the morning newspaper as something that starts tragically and ends happily, with assorted columnists and editorials mixed in.

The news services (such as the Associated Press) and the comics are two standardizing aspects of our culture that lead to an element of uniformity of information and sensibility. These national news services do press us into common molds more than we might imagine. This is because, to a great degree, our newspapers are not identifiably ideological and do not interpret the world in an obviously partisan way. In many other countries you can tell a person's political persuasion by what he or she reads. The chosen newspaper explains everything in terms of its identifiable ideology. We do not get a particularistic political ideology in American newspapers, though it might be argued that they all champion our own anti-ideological "ideology" through what has been called "Welfare/Warfare Capitalism" posing as nonjudgmental reporting.

The facts! That is what we want in the morning. We seldom think about the pressure facts exert upon us, for information (as the term suggests) "forms" us in subtle and powerful ways. Every morning we want to know what has transpired. We want revelations, we want explanations, and above all we want the truth, which we all have been taught "will make us free." There is even a sensuous pleasure involved in opening up the morning paper and reading it as we eat breakfast.

The morning paper is for those the Austrian novelist Robert Musil described as "possibilitarians," people who sense the future as somehow "open" and are confident of their potentialities. The reader of the evening newspaper is in a different position. Traditionally, evening newspapers are read by working-class people who don't have the time to read the paper in the morning. They may have listened to the news as they drive home and may also watch the news when they get home.

For them the evening newspaper is not a collection of revelations but rather a summation and recapitulation of the day's events—along with advertisements and the traditional entertainment features. The evening newspaper in the major urban areas is, increasingly, getting to be like the dodo bird—an anachronism. Evening newspapers have no place in the classless all-middle-class America that we are creating (or at least trying to create).

When the last evening newspaper dies, there seems little doubt that we will find out about it—in detail, that is—in our morning newspaper.

THIRTY-ONE

Breakfast

Breakfast is the most mundane meal in most cuisines. It means, literally, to "break" one's "fast," which presumably started the day before, after the evening meal. Midnight snackers have not fasted very long, but that is beside the point—they still eat breakfast. For many people, the time from the evening meal of the night before to breakfast is quite long.

Some people do, at times, have fancy breakfasts; others on weekends merge their breakfasts and lunches into brunches. Many people have "junk" breakfasts—coffee and donuts or, for those in a hurry, some kind of "instant" breakfast. But there is,

I would suggest, a classic American breakfast that is ubiquitous in America and that a typical person wanting a "big" breakfast would have.

The menu for this breakfast is as follows: orange juice, cereal with milk and sugar, bacon and eggs (and perhaps with pan-fried potatoes), toast and butter (with, perhaps, jam), coffee, cream, and sugar. There are, of course, all kinds of variations on this standard breakfast, but I will take it as the quintessential American big breakfast. This combination of dishes is found in most restaurants. (It is also now out of favor with nutritionists because of its fat content.)

I would like to "decipher" this meal and show what it represents. In order to do this we must find the fundamental elements in the meal and see how they are related. I am not concerned here specifically with what is eaten so much as with the hidden but meaningful relationships between the various items. In other words, what I am looking for is the "structure" of the meal, which may reveal some surprises when I deconstruct it. In this kind of investigation we do not look at the classic American breakfast as a meal but rather as a "system"—a collection of units or elements that are structured in some way that ties them together but that frequently is not evident. Another way of putting this is that there is a breakfast code and our mission is to "crack" this code.

In making my analysis, I assumed that there was some kind of a hidden structure in the classic American breakfast and started looking for the key that might unlock it. I worked on this problem first by drawing pictures of each of the items involved. Then I listed them: orange juice, coffee, cream, sugar, cornflakes, milk, bacon, eggs, and so on. For my first attempt at cracking the breakfast code I took the matter of whether each item was eaten hot or cold. Of the thirteen items in the classic American breakfast, eight are eaten cold and five are eaten hot. All the colors are earthy, warm ones: orange, brownish black, light brown, yellow, white, and so on. Color was another dead end in this particular case.

Perhaps, I thought, shape might reveal something. Most of the items had no shapes of their own but instead occupied the shape given by their containers: juice, coffee, cream, milk, sugar. So what? So nothing, I decided, and moved on to taste. But I found describing tastes to be impossible—other than in very general terms such as sweet, sour, or bitter. I abandoned taste, the way many of our food manufacturers have, and moved on to substances. What are we talking about, I asked myself? Fruits, cereals, dairy products, meats, and sugar. And what is sugar, I asked myself. The dictionary gave me my answer: "A sweet, crystalline substance . . . obtained chiefly from the juice of the sugar cane and sugar beet." Sugar is a liquid that became a solid.

That led me to consider a category I had not thought of earlier—namely, solids and liquids. When I ran my items through the solids or liquids category, nothing remarkable emerged. Juice, coffee, cream, and milk are liquids. And toast, cereal, eggs, bacon, and potatoes are solids. I couldn't find anything promising there. But there was something about this category that intrigued me.

Then it came to me. The fundamental matter was not whether something was a solid or a liquid but whether something had become *transformed* from solid to liquid or vice versa. It was only when I came upon the notion of transformations that I found anything interesting.

Let's start down the list. Orange juice is a solid that becomes a liquid. Coffee is a drink made from a solid—coffee beans. Sugar is a solid (sugar cane or beets) that becomes a liquid (juice) and then a solid again (sugar crystals). Eggs are liquid and become solid when cooked. And so forth. We find ourselves, ultimately, with four possibilities: some items are solids and become liquids and then become solids again; some items are liquids and become solids; some items are solids and become liquids; and some items maintain their identities as solids or liquids. The following lists show which items belong in which categories:

Solid to Liquid to Solid
  sugar, cornflakes (cereal)
Solid to Liquid
  orange juice, coffee, milk, cream
Liquid to Solid
  butter, eggs
Maintain Status
  preserves, bacon, potatoes, toast

In recent years, perhaps as a result of so much foreign travel, Americans have discovered espresso coffee—a coffee that is much richer and has a more complex flavor than the weak and watery percolator and drip coffee that used to be standard here. Actually, espresso has always been available, but until recently it was more or less confined to Italian restaurants and arty coffee houses in a few big cities. It is made by forcing hot water, under high pressure, through high-quality, finely ground coffee beans—a process that extracts the very essence of the beans. Espresso making also requires powerful and expensive espresso coffeemakers, which yield crema, a thin brown foam that appears when the coffee is made correctly with freshly ground beans.

Espresso also allows Americans to show their sense of refinement and discrimination and to order an almost bewildering number of variations: decaffeinated or with caffeine, black or with milk (nonfat, low fat, regular), hot or iced, liquid or frozen, lattes or cappuccinos, flavored or pure. An espresso craze, with an evangelical fervor, has swept the West Coast and has spread all over America. Coffeehouse franchises, suddenly, are everywhere. We even find gas stations (usually with espresso carts) and bookstores serving espresso.

Invented in Italy in 1905, espresso came to America, like many other Italian immigrants, to prosper. And it has. Of all the liquids we consume at breakfast, it is coffee, I would suggest, that has undergone the most radical and most fundamental changes. It has reinvented itself and has moved from being a lowly, and rather pedestrian, proletarian brew to a wildly popular petty-bourgeois yuppie beverage.

What we discover, then, is that breakfast is to a great degree a study in transformations. Is it not possible to assume that the people who consume this breakfast will believe, magically, in their power to transform themselves? Or that they can change their identities in a manner analogous to the transformations of some of the things they eat?

I have been assuming in this analysis that food is a kind of coded phenomenon. This idea is not original to me. Mary Douglas has written, in an essay titled "Deciphering a Meal," that "if food is treated as a code, the messages it encodes will be found in the pattern of social relations being expressed. The message is about different degrees of hierarchy, inclusion and exclusion, boundaries and transactions across boundaries" (1975, 249).

In a society that sees itself as a classless all-middle-class society, it must be possible for people to escape their original class identities and become middle class. The problem that merging the classes causes is that one loses something of one's original identity. There is a psychic cost to be paid for this. The message of the classic American breakfast is that disguise is efficacious and transformation is possible. We believe that, like the breakfasts we eat, we can transform ourselves into anyone or anything we wish. The classic American breakfast is a high-protein (and also a highly protean) meal.

THIRTY-TWO

The Toaster

The existence of the toaster implies the existence of sliced bread, for that is what one uses in a toaster. And sliced bread itself implies a certain kind of bread: bread that has a particular form or shape most practical for slicing. Bread has been mechanized and standardized and is no longer a product with an irregular shape; as it is manufactured it no longer need be touched by human hands.

This does not mean that we do not have other kinds of bread. We do, but generally they cost more than the standard loaf of white or whole-grain bread. These "touched by human hands" breads tend to be ethnic—French, Italian, Jewish, Russian—and are generally irregular in shape and often have a crust.

The toaster is part of a system and only has significance relative to the wrapped, baked-in-the-pan, thin-crusted bread that can be used in it. One problem with this bread is that it is very soft and spongy. This is the result of the mechanization of bread, described by Siegfried Giedion in *Mechanization Takes Command* as follows:

> The bread of full mechanization has the resiliency of a rubber sponge. When squeezed it returns to its former shape. The loaf becomes constantly whiter, more elastic, and frothier. . . . Since mechanization, it has often been pointed out, white bread has become much richer in fats, milk, and sugar. But these are added largely to stimulate sales by heightening the loaf's eye-appeal. The shortenings used in bread, a leading authority states, are "primarily for the purpose of imparting desirable tender eating or chewing qualities to the finished product." They produce the "soft velvet crumb," a cake-like structure, so that the bread is half-masticated, as it were, before reaching the mouth. (1969, 193)

Giedion has also described this bread as neither bread nor cake but something halfway between the two. This kind of bread is a highly rationalized product designed to maximize profit for the baker. Consumers have had to be "taught" to like this kind of bread, and this was, no doubt, part of the process of "Americanization" that many ethnic immigrant groups underwent, a way of repudiating one's ethnic identity and non-Americanness. (There are, of course, new developments taking place. In large cities one can get "handbaked" breads that are more substantial and more interesting. And even packaged bread seems to be changing, so that more whole-grain breads are available as alternatives to the standard loaf of white bread.) One thing the toaster does is change the nature of this bread, giving it a color, making it firmer and easier to handle.

An interesting philosophical problem is raised by the toaster. What is toast—the product of a process or the process itself? That is, does bread become toast (and change its identity somehow), or do we toast bread and thereby only modify its character slightly? Is toast bread that has been processed (toasted) or changed (made into toast)?

Obviously, we start off with a piece of bread—and for our purposes, let us assume that we have the standard loaf of sliced bread with its thin crust. The question is whether we end up with a variation of the piece of sliced bread or something that is different. In terms of the dynamics of American culture, I suggest that we would like to think that toast is something different from bread itself. That is, the process involves a major transformation (in the same way that grinding a steak turns it into hamburger). We believe in the power of change and in our ability to change our circumstance and status.

This kind of white bread may be the perfect product for the middle classes, standing midway, as they do, between the upper classes and the working classes. Their bread, if Giedion is right, is midway between traditional bread and cake (neither one nor the other). Toast may suggest, unconsciously, a transformation to a higher status. The working classes eat their crusts of bread; the elites "take toast and tea."

The toaster has also led to the development of new products, the most pernicious of which is probably the Pop-Tart, meant to be "baked" in the toaster as a mechanized kind of sweet roll. The Pop-Tart is a new food product and a relatively successful one, though its sweetness makes it appealing mostly to young children. Toasters themselves have undergone transformations. Older versions required the person making the toast to flip the toast over when one side was done—the toast had to be watched. Then came the "pop" toaster, which toasts bread to whatever degree of lightness or darkness one wants, then pops it up. In the earlier versions of the pop toaster one had to depress the bread using some kind of knob or lever, but the most advanced form of toaster now has a mechanism that takes care of that. One merely inserts the bread in the opening in the toaster and it sinks slowly out of sight to reemerge, almost magically, when it has become toast.

For large families there are toasters that can toast four slices of bread at a time to different degrees of darkness. Thus a toaster can be spewing out light, medium, and dark toast more or less at the same time. Heat sensors in the toaster measure the temperature and the moisture content of the bread and pop it up at the proper moment. (Making toast on the basis of timers is old-fashioned and low tech.)

Ultimately, the toaster is an apology for the quality of our bread. It attempts, heroically, to transform the semisweet, characterless "plastic" packaged bread that we have been taught to love into something more palatable and more manageable. Perhaps our handling this bread and warming it up gives us a sense that the bread now has a human touch to it, is not an abstract, almost unreal product. The toaster represents a heroic attempt to redeem our packaged bread, to redeem the unredeemable. But the toaster, despite its high-tech functions, is doomed to the continual repetition of (symbolically speaking) Adam and Eve's fall, for an unregenerate bread cannot be saved.

Every piece of toast is a tragedy.

THIRTY-THREE
Garbage Disposals

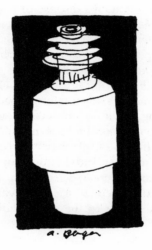

The garbage (or "food waste") disposal is a standard feature in houses nowadays and has been for many years. It is an electro-mechanical hydraulic device that grinds food wastes into mush that can then be washed down the drain.

These devices are somewhat analogous to the human digestive system, except that we have chemical solutions to decompose our food and the disposal has a grinding chamber and shredder plates. We have teeth for grinding and a stomach that

159

acts as a "dissolving chamber," but, unlike the disposal, we consume food—it consumes "waste." It also contains its own toilet, so to speak, whereas we must deposit our wastes in a separate device. The waste disposal is a combination stomach and
digestive system.

Waste must be defined here as food we do not wish to eat, not
food that cannot be eaten. We dispose of a great deal of good
food, actually: food left on our plates because we took too
much or food we leave because we don't like it, and so on. The
garbage disposal represents a major change in psychology relative to the matter of garbage. Before the disposal we kept
garbage but "contained" it and isolated it. Garbage, then, had
a place in our scheme of things. It was smelly and perhaps at
times even disgusting, but it forced us to recognize that fact that
there is waste in life and that living things ultimately decay.

It might be said that we "tolerated" garbage even if we did
not like having it around. And it stunk, making its presence
known. But America, a sacred society, a paradisiacal entity (as
it sees itself), is not supposed to be a place where things (or people) stink, and so we took to the garbage disposal with great
eagerness.

Now it is possible for us to relate to garbage in a different
way. We no longer contain and separate ourselves from this pollution but annihilate it. There are strong emotions here, remnants of morbid residues (psychological garbage) that are
behind our feelings of disgust for garbage. Garbage generates
anxieties in us, for we see or interpret garbage as death.

And the smell of garbage makes us think of the smell of putri-
fying corpses (or, more precisely, what we imagine the smell
would be like, since most of us have never smelled a real
corpse). It is an aspect of life that we wish to put out of mind
and can do so, for with the waste disposal we annihilate
garbage and its smell, and with that the thought of death. In a
sense we try to do the same with death itself. Death is not seen

as that which makes life meaningful and gives it significance but as something disgusting that must be kept away from consciousness.

Perhaps we even delude ourselves into thinking that we are "disposing of" death with these devices. At least they enable us to make a step in the right direction, for we no longer have to bother with garbage and no longer need tolerate its smell, or even the knowledge of its existence in some shed.

Garbage, of course, is a concept, a category. Something is good food, but at some point it "becomes" garbage and is then no longer edible. Or desirable. But when does a piece of fruit, for example, move from being ripe to being garbage? In many cases it is hard to know. Our readiness to assign food to the garbage category is a reflection, in part, of our economic affluence. When one is rich, defining something as garbage is much easier than when one is poor.

There is also a cultural bias here. As a result of our Puritan background, we are very much concerned about the purity of our food. Think of the difference here, for example, between the American mania for fresh, pure foods and the Mexican passion for *huitlacoche,* a diseased form of corn that has the additional problem of being black. Ironically, much of our "pure" food is full of chemical products that are of questionable value as far as our health is concerned, but that is another matter. Chemical additives are not classified as "garbage" or dangerous, except by a small proportion of people who eat only organic products (though we are increasingly becoming wary of the additives in food). For them, for those who eat only organic foods, most of the food that Americans eat is contaminated and thus "garbage."

Using a waste disposal generates a number of different emotions: hatred and rage against garbage that signifies pollution and death, and exhilaration at having vanquished death, if only for the moment. When we see the garbage disposal as more than one more household gadget but rather as something that involves us intimately and directly with universal problems, such as how to deal with pollution, we can understand why disposals might have deep psychological meanings that are not apparent.

The disposal is part of the vast apparatus in contemporary American life for keeping things in their place, for preventing decay and pollution from spreading, for dealing with "dirty" or disgusting things. To see the garbage disposal as nothing more than a convenience for housewives is to fail to see the profound significance of this appliance and underestimate its role in contemporary American culture. Perhaps the grim reaper is an antiquated image. Could it be that when death comes for us now, he too takes advantage of the latest technology and dumps us into some gigantic waste disposal?

THIRTY-FOUR

Dishwashers

A number of years ago a company that manufactured dish-washers advertised them with the theme, "Get a dishwasher . . . don't be one." The theme was particularly apt because in recent years middle-class families have not been able to afford (or even find) servants to do the "dirty" work (of everyday living). The

 **Dishwashers**

housewife, more than anyone else in the family, has ended up doing what servants used to do.

That's why dishwashers are so important.

They are mechanical devices that promise to liberate the housewife from one more unpleasant and endlessly occurring task—cleaning the dishes after meals. In addition, the dishwasher promises to do a better job of cleaning the dishes than could be done by hand. The dishwasher uses very hot water and detergents that are too caustic for human hands. Dishwashing liquids, which are used when people do the dishes by hand, face a serious problem: The soaps must be "gentle" on the skin so women can continue to be glamour queens with soft and beautiful hands, and yet the soaps must be powerful so women can do the dishes quickly and easily. (We know that in the world of television commercials it is women who do the dishes, for they are the ones to whom the appeals are made all the time. Men don't usually worry about having soft hands.)

Thus the dishwasher promises liberation from drudgery and asepsis at the same time—dishes that are clean and germ-free. The dishwasher duplicates what humans do when they wash dishes, but with a vengeance. The dishes are lashed with steaming hot water that is full of a powerful detergent, which process is continued several times until they are rinsed and can be subjected to heat to dry them.

Of course the liberation they promise the housewife is only partial. Someone must load and unload the dishwasher and in some cases rinse the dishes before putting them in the dishwasher. Still, it is a great improvement over doing the dishes by hand all the time.

The dishwasher symbolizes, perhaps more than any other appliance, the Sisyphean nature of housework. Like Sisyphus and his boulder, one never finishes with washing dishes, for no sooner are the dishes cleaned and emptied from the dishwasher

164

and stacked than they are used and dirtied again. The cycle repeats itself every day, many times a day, endlessly.

This is because the dishwasher is symbolically tied, ultimately, to the human digestive system. We are constantly eating, which means we are continually dirtying dishes. Dietitians no longer talk about three meals per day as a matter of fact but use terms like "food experiences," for we graze—we eat a number of times during the day and night. Dirty plates are signs, then, of our having eaten, and sometimes there are scraps of food, bits of congealed fat, and crumbs on the plates to bother us even more.

We do not wish to be reminded of our appetites (for food or other things), so dirty plates are psychologically disturbing. They can be devastating. They remind us that we are human, that we must continually eat in order to live, and that like all living things we will eventually die. How convenient it is then to have this big box in the kitchen into which we can load the plates, cups, silverware, and pots and pans we have "dirtied" and get them out of sight at least, if not out of mind.

An interesting question suggests itself here. Why do we describe dishes that we've just eaten from as "dirty"? Why do we use that term? Are dishes that were clean and upon which we've placed good food suddenly now dirty? Obviously we are using the word "dirty" in a special way. We define dirty—here and elsewhere—not positively, as in "with dirt," but negatively. Something is dirty when it is no longer clean, or in this case unused.

We discover, then, an interesting perspective on our attitudes toward cleanliness. Dirty is not seen as the opposite of clean. Dirtiness is the negation of "not used yet," which is posited, then, as the original state. Dirtiness is a lack of cleanliness, a kind of deficiency that may characterize something. A clean plate (once it has been used for a piece of toast, for example) becomes classified as dirty or "used," no longer pure. The fact that we call dishes dirty suggests almost a kind of moral reprobation of them. It also suggests an impoverishment in our language and classification system for separating the clean from the unclean or nonclean. Our attitudes toward pollution, which are in turn connected to our beliefs about society, sexuality, and disease, are reflected in the way we think about our "dirty" dishes.

With our dishes as with other kinds of pollution, our answer is to separate, put out of sight, attempt to purify and rehabilitate. This is easily accomplished, in the case of dishes, with the dishwasher. In other situations, when we are dealing with "dirty" old people, or "dirty" crooks, or "dirty" Jews, the situation is more complicated.

Trash Compactors

It was Parmenides who refuted motion, and it is the trash compactor that strives to make Parmenides's theory a reality. Parmenides started with a simple notion: "Nothing cannot exist," he argued. "Whatever is, is and whatever is not, is not." From this simple start he demolished the concept of motion. The reasoning is clear.

If nothing cannot exist, everything must have the same density. If this were not true, one could compress less dense material until it had the density of the most dense material, but that would leave a residue of nothing, which cannot exist. Motion, remember, involves the passage of dense objects or relatively dense objects through less dense objects, for example the human body moving through air or water. If everything has the same density there cannot be motion, and we are stuck, so to speak (at least in theory), wherever we find ourselves.

Obviously, this theory is both logical and incorrect, for motion is possible in the real world. Not all objects have the same density and not all *can* have the same density. And this is where the trash compactor comes in.

It is very much a Parmenidesian appliance and exists to compress trash or rubbish into a uniform (or relatively uniform) mass. By exerting great pressure on trash it creates a small block of junk, imposing order and regularity on what is a random collection of objects whose only characteristic in common is that they are all being thrown away. This matter of imposing form (in this case a relatively geometrical one) on what is formless is a common theme in human behavior. The existence of the trash compactor is an enigma. What need do we have for this domestic version of the garbage truck? Why bother to give shape to rubbish?

In part the trash compactor reflects a general anxiety we feel about the way we are generating and perhaps being inundated by rubbish. Newspaper articles point out that the average person in America generates so many pounds of paper waste, so many pounds of glass waste, so many pounds of plastic waste, and so on, in a given day and point out that we are running out of space to bury our garbage and rubbish. Unless we erect costly and sophisticated plants to recycle our paper, glass, and metal wastes we will soon run out of space and some kind of an incredible "rubbish-lock" will occur.

There will be so much rubbish that we won't be able to move. Parmenides may have "proved" that, logically speaking, motion is impossible, but we fear we will, as a result of our prodigiously wasteful lifestyle, *make* motion impossible. The trash compactor, by reducing the bulk of rubbish, by pressing it into a neat little package, helps avoid "rubbish-lock." It is our own personal contribution to the good society.

Actually, there is some question about what rubbish actually is. Michael Thompson, in a fascinating book titled *Rubbish Theory*, points out that rubbish is a social concept, that different groups of people have different views of what is and what isn't rubbish. As he writes in the book, "The basic idea is that physical objects have certain important properties imposed on them as a result of the processes of human social life, and, conversely, that if these properties were not conferred upon them then human social life would not be possible. Since people are physical objects, they too are subject to the same process. Nor does it stop here. Ideas, since they must always be generated and communicated in a social context, are also constrained so as to become . . . thinglike" (1979, 77).

Thompson uses this notion to deal with a variety of sociological, economic, and political matters. We know also that there is a new discipline (if one can call it that) known as "garbageology," which makes systematic and highly sophisticated studies of people's garbage to gain data on how they live. When we know what people have eaten and used and thrown away, we know a lot about people—more than we find out when we ask them to answer questions, if the garbageologists are correct. Garbage doesn't lie, but people often do.

The trash compactor is one more power appliance found in the kitchen and under the control, generally, of women. It is probably the most powerful of the home appliances and the one that transforms matter the most profoundly. The trash compactor helps women "contain" the continual disorder in which they find themselves and order the world, give it shape and regularity.

It is a bizarre mechanical imitation of the "constrictions" women undergo when they give birth. Except that they give birth to children, not packages of compressed rubbish. For some extreme environmentalists, however, as Thompson points out, "children are pollution," so the difference between giving birth and using a trash compactor is not that great—for some people and in some respects. "For some people and in some respects" is about all social scientists seem to be able to tell us about anything, which is why many people think social science is, itself, all too often rubbish.

In "To His Coy Mistress," Andrew Marvell suggested,

> *Let us roll all our strength and all*
> *Our sweetness up into one ball*
> *And tear our pleasures with rough strife*
> *Thorough the iron gates of life*

Could Marvell have been anticipating the trash compactor?

THIRTY-SIX

Mail

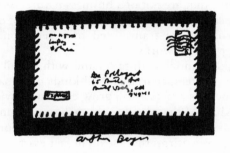

Receiving good mail is one of life's great pleasures. Too bad most of don't get many personal letters anymore. It seems that the practice of maintaining personal correspondences is waning and most of the interpersonal communication we get is electronic—from the telephone, from radios and television sets, on tapes or records, or from computers. (The development of electronic mail, or e-mail, is a phenomenon that counters this tendency, but it is not available to everyone; one must have a computer, a modem, and be connected to some electronic network.)

What mail we do get is frequently described as "junk," which means unsolicited and impersonal. This is mail that tries to sell us something or get us to do something. Mail, I would suggest, can be classified into the following categories: personal mail, junk mail, bills, and publications. The personal mail category may be too broad, actually, in that some personal mail has to do with business, so it might be more accurate to add "private correspondence" to our list, a term we will reserve for letters between people that are not of a business nature. As postal rates go up and electronic technology improves, much of our business mail will probably be transmitted over telephone lines and through computer networks.

It is being done now, with faxes and with e-mail. It is possible to transmit letters, charts, and all kinds of visual data over the phone, and this practice will grow even more widespread in the future. Most of the mail we get at home is junk mail and bills. Since one of the functions of private correspondence is to remind us (or to reaffirm) that we do in fact exist and have relationships with others, and since we seldom write to one another, bills now have taken over this job to a great degree. We might modify Descartes's maxim *credo ergo sum* to *credito ergo sum*, which can be translated, roughly, as "I have credit, therefore I exist." Bills exist in a limbo halfway between junk mail (which, thanks to the computer, is often pseudopersonal) and private correspondence; bills mediate between organizations and our personal lives (and our bank accounts).

As such, they do not give us anywhere near as much pleasure as does a letter from a friend. Private correspondence usually generates a great deal of psychological pleasure: Every letter is pregnant with hope and possibility. Letters are also tangible. Of all letters, airmail letters from abroad are the most visually stimulating and exciting. They come with elaborate stripings on the envelope, are often covered with beautiful stamps, and suggest that one is, somehow, "world class."

I have suggested that letters serve an existential function and confirm the fact that we exist. They also do other things. For in personal correspondences, aside from getting news about those we care about or love, we also get insights about ourselves (as well as advice, suggestions, consolations, and sometimes bad news). Writing is a means of self-discovery and self-disclosure. This explains why letter writing is so difficult for many people—they are afraid to write lest they "give themselves away" somehow.

Letters are fragments of ongoing autobiographies and are records of a person's growth and development (or the lack of it) over the years. Some letters even have literary value and are, in certain cases, published. So the letter must be seen as more than a simple communication. Letter writing is an art form that can lead to astonishing and valuable creations.

Because mail bears such a heavy existential burden, people feel very anxious about mail—without knowing why. When mail deliveries are late we get terribly upset, though we may not be expecting anything at all. But there might be a letter, and one letter can make all the difference in the world. (For writers, waiting for the mail—which means waiting to hear what agents, editors, and all kinds of other people have decided—is often absolutely hellish.)

We also tend to measure the decline in the quality of our lives by the kind of mail service we get and, related to that, by the rise in the price of stamps. The post office is a symbol of dedication and determination. We all know the motto of the United States Postal Service, which will "brave sleet and snow" in the performance of its duties. And there is something absolutely wonderful about being able to drop a letter in a mailbox and know, with reasonable certainty, that it will be delivered just about any place in the world.

The mail systems of the world suggest the possibility of worldwide cooperation and give us reason to be hopeful. And the letters we get remind us that someone, somewhere, cares about us. Or about our money.

PART 3
Conclusion

The world is simply ridiculous if one looks at it from the technical point of view. It is unpractical in all that concerns the relations between human beings, and in the highest degree uneconomical and inexact in its methods. And anyone who is in the habit of dealing with his affairs by means of a slide-rule finds that a good half of all human assertions cannot be taken seriously. A slide-rule consists of two incredibly ingeniously combined systems of figures and divisions; a slide-rule consists of two little white enamelled rods, the cross-section of which is a flat trapezium, which slide into each other, a device by the aid of which one can instantly solve the most complicated problems, without wasting any thought on the matter; a slide-rule is a little symbol that one carries in one's breast pocket, feeling it as a hard white line over one's heart. If one owns a slide-rule and someone comes along with large assertions or grand feelings, one says: "Just a moment, please—first of all let's work out the margin of error and the approximate value of the thing!"

—Robert Musil,
The Man Without Qualities

Myth, Culture, and Everyday Life

The analysis of everyday life I made in *Bloom's Morning* represents an effort on my part to look behind what seem to be trivial and uninteresting rituals and objects in our everyday lives and discover, with each topic analyzed, some illuminating insight. Each chapter represents, then, an attempt at an epiphany, a search on my part for some kind of a "luminous" revelation that would help my readers see everything from clock radios to the morning mail differently.

Defamiliarizing and Making Strange

Some may object that I have not really discovered anything, and that *Bloom's Morning* is closer to a dream than to a sociocultural or sociosemiotic analysis; that is, I have "read" into our everyday rituals and the objects we use in them my own wild ideas, personal fantasies, or whatever else you might wish to call them. This is a typical criticism that all who interpret things face: Namely, it is asserted by those who disagree with the interpretation or the methodology of analysis used that the interpreters are reading in things that aren't in the texts, stories, objects being analyzed—what you will. I will leave that judgment, whether my essays represent invention or discovery, for my readers.

My method in part is to defamiliarize (*ostranenie* in Russian, or "make strange") everyday life. Victor Shklovsky, the Russian formalist critic, talks about this process in his essay "Art as Technique"(Lodge 1988, 16–30). In this essay he points out that as we become habituated to things, the way we relate to them becomes automatic and the objects that are part of our lives become more or less invisible. He calls this process of over-automatizing objects "algebrization" and says we use it because it permits us to achieve the greatest economies in our perceptive efforts. We don't have to bother looking at or thinking about the things that are familiar to us or that we have included in our daily routines and rituals.

He quotes from Leo Tolstoy's diary:

> I was cleaning a room and, meandering about, approached the divan and couldn't remember whether or not I had dusted it. Since these movements are habitual and unconscious, I could not remember and felt that it was impossible to remember—so that if I had dusted it and forgot— that is, had acted unconsciously, then it was the same as if I had not. If some conscious person had been watching, then the fact could be established. If, however, no one was looking, or looking on unconsciously, if the whole complex lives of many people go on unconsciously, then such lives are as if they had never been. (Lodge 1988, 20)

"If the whole complex lives of many people go on unconsciously, then such lives are as if they had never been." What a line! And what a remarkable insight. Without thinking about it or recognizing what we are doing, Tolstoy tells us, we dream-walk through much of our everyday lives.

This situation leads Shklovsky to suggest that "habitualization devours work, clothes, furniture, one's wife, and the fear of war." What he describes as being habitualized, the realm of the routinized, I think of as everyday life, which can also be considered the realm of the unconsciously repeated. Shklovsky counters everyday life with art. What art does, Shklovsky adds, is make objects unfamiliar; it defamiliarizes them, makes them strange.

He adds an important insight: One of the ways art works is to increase the amount of time we spend perceiving objects. Art helps deautomatize perception, and that is precisely what I have tried to do in *Bloom's Morning*—make the familiar strange, force us to look more carefully at that which we consider to be trivial and uninteresting. I have given common objects more than the cursory glance most people give them and, using a variety of methods and techniques from aesthetics to psychoanalytic theory, have tried to surprise my readers, have tried to find the marvelous that is hidden in the mundane.

In writing about my subjects I confess to some tricks—exaggeration, irony, absurdity, wild analogies, trying to shock, or adopting (in some cases) a pose of innocence—that is, doing whatever I felt was necessary to make readers perceive, examine, and speculate for a moment about what habituation had rendered invisible to them in their everyday lives. I've put on a straight face but have written whimsically in many cases. And so, I have gone searching for latent functions and repetition compulsions, and I have, using a variety of approaches, uncovered the hidden values and beliefs that are attached to the objects we use and the rituals we follow in our everyday lives.

Bloom's Everyday Life Is Not
Everyone's Everyday Life

The everyday life I investigated in *Bloom's Morning* is that of an ideal-type hero—a middle-aged, middle-class white male living in an urban setting: not in Dublin, but in some analogue to it in the United States of America. There are, of course, many different everyday lives or styles of everyday life depending upon everything from one's gender and ethnicity and skin color to one's socioeconomic class and geographical location in the United States. Everyday life in New Orleans is different from everyday life in Boston or Iowa City, Iowa. And the everyday life of people who are poor is different from that of people who are middle class, and *their* everyday lives are different from those of the extremely wealthy.

But there are some commonalties nevertheless. Men all over the United States do use clock radios to wake up, wear underwear, take showers, brush their teeth (though not always with gel toothpastes), shave, and have (on occasion) orange juice, cereal and milk, toast, and bacon and eggs for breakfast (though our fear of cholesterol is changing the so-called classic or typical American breakfast). So my Leopold Bloom may, in a number of respects, be typical or representative. And although some people in the United States of America may eat *congee* for breakfast, others croissants and cappuccinos, and others steak and eggs, it is possible to say that Bloom, and all those like him, is fairly representative and typical, or perhaps even archetypical.

The United States has so many geographical regions with separate cultural identities that it is difficult to make generalizations about what Americans like or are like. We have a number of regions with distinct identities, for instance the East Coast, the Midwest, the Pacific Northwest (Arcadia), the Deep South, the Southwest (Mexicali), and the Far West. (Ironically, San

Francisco, which is west of Montana and Colorado, is more eastern than they are. And so is Los Angeles, though it is rapidly turning into an American province of Mexico.)

And we have any number of different subcultures, ethnic communities, and religious groups and are split in so many ways that it is very difficult to make any generalizations that cover everyone in the country—except, perhaps, for the generalization that no generalizations are possible or that, at the highest level of abstraction, certain values seem to be dominant in people raised in the United States (or in those who come here and adopt these values and beliefs): individualism, egalitarianism, achievement, democracy, and so on. Thus, I would argue that although Bloom is not completely representative, we can see in his everyday life, in the objects that are part of it, and in the activities he engages in, reflections that are not too distorted of each of ours.

On Myth, History, the Elite Arts, Popular Culture, and Everyday Life

A number of years ago I developed an exercise based on a metaphor for students in my popular culture courses: I suggested that culture is like an onion and that as we peel away everyday life, we come to popular culture; when we peel *it* away, we find elite culture; when we peel *it* away, we find historical experience, and at the core of the onion we find myth. This is illustrated in the drawing on the next page.

The exercise involved having students take a myth and see how it manifested itself in some historical event, in some texts in the elite arts, some texts in popular culture, and in everyday life.

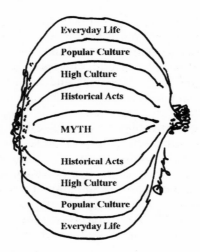

In this postmodern era it is not fashionable to separate elite arts and the popular arts, but let us do so here for didactic purposes.

I assume also, for the purpose of the exercise, that there is a difference between popular culture (or mass-mediated culture) and everyday life, though popular culture and everyday lives may be and probably are parts of the same thing. Assuming some kind of a difference for heuristic purposes, we know that our everyday lives are full of, if not dominated by, popular culture and are shaped by it as well. (And, conversely, much of our popular culture is about our everyday lives, if you think about it: commercials for products, situation comedies, many dramas, and so on.)

We listen to the radio for several hours a day while we are getting washed, having breakfast, and commuting—in other words, living our everyday lives. And the average American, researchers tell us, watches close to four hours of television each day, so television can be said to dominate the nonworking portions of our everyday lives. To this accounting you must add reading newspapers, magazines, and books and listening to records. You discover that much of our leisure time (that is, the nonwork part of our everyday lives) is spent immersed in mass media, and it, in turn, is about our everyday lives. Much of what we watch on television takes the form of narrative, but so does everyday life.

Listen to people chatting. Their conversations are full of "I said, he said, she said, they said" comments. Bloom's everyday life, remember, was described in terms of a narrative. Then each element of his life—each object he used, each artifact he was involved with, each daily ritual he practiced—was subjected to inspection, analysis, and interpretation. We tend to think of our lives as formless for the most part because they are so familiar to us. But they can be seen as, and really are, narratives: That is, they have a linear structure and involve our doing varying tasks. It may be that the personal narrative we each live, our everyday life, is repeated so often that it loses its contours and identity, but it is possible to argue that our everyday lives are narratives that are related to the narratives we see, read about, or hear about in the media. And they, we realize, are often versions or modifications of ancient narratives.

Sisyphus and Everyday Life

If everyday life is that realm that is infinitely repeatable, we can see without pushing things too hard that the myth of Sisyphus has a relevance to everyday life. For it is Sisyphus's fate to push a stone up a mountain, and just before he reaches the top the stone rolls down to the bottom of the mountain. Sisyphus must spend eternity doing the same fruitless thing over and over again. Let us look at the areas dealt with in my onion of culture metaphor: a myth, historical events, elite arts, popular culture, and everyday life.

Sisyphus's life, that is, the "myth" of Sisyphus, can be seen as a metaphor for our everyday lives, for, like him, most of us spend our lives doing the same thing over and over again, even if we escape on weekends and holidays from our routines and our work (though we seldom escape from the fundamentals of everyday life—sleeping, fornicating, cleaning ourselves, eating, digesting, and defecating, if we are to reduce life to its most elementary physiological functions). Sisyphus is, then, a paradigmatic figure whose life is to a considerable degree a model for our everyday lives.

In the realm of history, we might argue that the seemingly endless cycle of wars and peace settlements, sometimes between different countries and sometimes between factions in a single country, has a Sisyphean dimension to it. Human beings seem unable to escape from this cycle, and even though we've been able to avoid a third world war, there are something like forty wars being waged in different countries around the world in the 1990s.

In elite culture, let me suggest a novel such as Albert Camus's *The Myth of Sisyphus,* or something more contemporary, such as Nicholson Baker's *The Mezzanine.* Although not focused immediately on the repetitiousness of daily life, *The Mezzanine* is focused on the trivial matters we concern ourselves with as we lead our everyday lives. Serial music and the work of various minimalist composers may also be connected to this overarching myth. We can also see *The Bald Soprano* as Sisyphean, for as soon as the play ends we find it repeating itself with the performers playing the Martins returning as the Smiths, so that in theory the play keeps repeating, endlessly. Ionesco used an English-language phrase book as the basis of his play—and the purpose of such conversation guides is the matter of helping us deal with our everyday needs.

In popular culture, industrial music and many rock lyrics are repetitious and Sisyphean in nature. Soap operas also have this quality: Their characters face one problem after another—endlessly, it seems. (Some soaps have been going on for thirty years.) Any of the iterative arts, such as comic strips, have this quality and might be described as even more Sisyphean than soaps, since some comics have been running for sixty or eighty years. A classic example would be *Krazy Kat*, in which Ignatz Mouse spent more than thirty years trying to "bean" Krazy with a brick while Offissa Pupp tried to prevent him from doing so.

And then in the realm of everyday life there are the routines and rituals that shape our lives: setting the alarm system on our clock radios, reading the morning paper as we have our breakfast, setting off to work at a particular time, and so on, endlessly—except for the weekends and our vacations, when we escape these weekday routines and substitute others (weekend routines: sleeping late, going to religious services, partying, and so on).

We live our daily lives immersed in the world of the mundane, but much of what we do is connected, though we are generally not aware of it, to camouflaged myths and desacralized rituals. Only at certain moments—at New Year's Eve parties, at weddings, at religious holidays and festive celebrations—do we dimly perceive, perhaps, that our actions are connected to something beyond the moment—to natural phenomena, to another realm—namely, the realm of the sacred.

The Sacred and the Profane

This leads us to the topic that is at the highest level in our typology: myth. Myths are commonly described as sacred narratives, stories about paradigmatic heroes and heroines that help shape our consciousness. As Mark Shorer has explained things:

"Myths are the instrument by which we continually struggle to make our experience intelligible to ourselves. A myth is a large controlling image that gives philosophical meaning to the facts of ordinary life. These myths, operating generally below the level of awareness, function as models and as a means of explaining everyday life to people" (Murray 1968, 355).

Mircea Eliade argues in *The Sacred and the Profane* that modern profane man is profoundly affected by myth, even though he doesn't recognize this to be the case. As Eliade writes, "But the modern man who feels and claims that he is nonreligious still retains a large stock of camouflaged myths and degenerated rituals. As we remarked earlier, the festivities that go with the New Year or taking up residence in a new house, though laicized, still exhibit the structure of a ritual of renewal. The same phenomenon is observable in the merrymaking that accompanies a marriage or the birth of a child or obtaining a new position or a social advancement, and so on" (1961, 204–205).

He continues his analysis of this topic with a discussion of the cinema and the way this "dream factory" uses various mythological motifs—fights between heroes and monsters, combats and ordeals of initiation, exemplary heroes and heroines, and so on. Films and other such narratives are, for Eliade, functional alternatives of the recitations of myths that took place in archaic communities and the recitation of oral literature that still takes place in certain communities. Eliade also adds that reading enables one to escape from time (and "kill time") the way myths used to enable people to emerge *from* time in the old days.

Thus, there is good reason to argue that much of what we do in our everyday lives is, without our being aware of it or recognizing its "sacred" content, a camouflaged and secularized version of sacred rituals that are connected, themselves, to ancient myths. This applies also to time, for Eliade distinguished between profane time, which passes, and sacred time, generally tied to festivities, which is circular, recoverable, repeatable, never changing, and never exhausted. Is it not possible that the infinite repeatability of everyday life, the seemingly endless repetition of being wakened, cleaning oneself, dressing, eating, going off to work, coming home, etc., etc., is connected, somehow, to sacred time? That everyday life, which is the realm of profane time, gains its definition by being different from sacred time, by being interrupted by it on a regular basis (carnivals, religious holidays, and so on, which represent a return to sacred time and ancient rituals)?

It is reasonable to suggest, I believe, that ancient myths do have some connection with our everyday lives and that many of the things we do are connected, even if we generally don't see these connections to a number of central myths—at least in the Western world, which is the context for discussing American culture.

The Culture of Consumption

We all must have some reasons to explain and justify what we do. In ancient times, if Eliade is correct, we had sacred rites (and the objects connected with them) to order our days and explain our activities. In the absence of the sacred as the foundation for our actions, we needed a substitute and have found a functional alternative to justify our activities and "explain" what is important in life, and that alternative is status as it is reflected in consumer culture.

Everyday life is the dominant area of contention in contemporary societies as advertisers fight for our attention and our money. This is because our everyday lives are so directly connected with purchasing and using the products that our consumer culture creates—whether it is breakfast cereals or paper diapers or hundred-dollar athletic shoes or automobiles. As

Karl Marx pointed out, "Every man speculates upon creating a *new* need in another in order to force him to a new sacrifice, to place him in a new dependence, and to entice him into a new pleasure and thereby economic ruin. Everyone tries to establish over others an *alien* power in order to find there the satisfaction of his own egoistic need" (Fromm 1962, 50).

The world of consumer culture is one of new needs tied always to the engine of desire (which is limitless and insatiable and, as our advertising agencies have discovered, easily stimulated). We all have real needs, for food and shelter and clothing, but these real needs are buried under an avalanche of false or invented "needs" that the advertising world creates in us.

Everything we buy involves a choice, and every choice involves the acceptance of one plea by an advertiser and the rejection of other pleas by other advertisers. Even if we decide to purchase a product on the basis of price, there are often several competing products at the same price. Why then do we buy one product rather than another? Advertisers will tell us they don't know. All they do, as they often put it, is "run flags up flagpoles and see whether anyone salutes."

Marx's use of the word "alien" is significant, for it can be argued that the alienation Marxists see as part of bourgeois societies is functional for those who control the economy. It is the alienation and sense that one is a commodity, and therefore nothing, that helps generate the consumer lust one finds in consumer cultures. It is the sense of alienation and estrangement from oneself that leads people to buy all the products they do— in the hope of an ideal, namely, a better life for themselves and those they love.

Manufacturers have learned to exploit human sexuality through the design of the objects they create, through the advertisements they use, and even through the aestheticization and sexualization of the stores in which products are sold. Many of the objects we purchase have an aesthetic and sexual dimension to them in terms of their functions and the way they are designed, and to this we must add the metonymic sexualization layered on them by advertising agencies. We transfer our sexual appetites, so to speak, from persons to manufactured artifacts and objects—objects we come to "desire" and we wish to "possess," terms that have direct sexual implications.

The focus in consumer cultures on private spending, on buying goods for one's own purposes, takes our attention away from the need for public expenditures, for money spent for the good of everyone in society. The world of consumer culture is a privatistic and narcissistic one. We are not, like Narcissus, doomed forever to look at a reflection of ourselves in a stream; we escape from time to time, but only so we can look at ourselves in our mirrors later with our new purchases—everything from a new outfit to a new face. Narcissus, we must remember, was an alienated person so in love with his reflected image in a stream that he could not take his eyes off his own face, and thus, lovesick, he died.

The myth of Narcissus is an important one. He was so beautiful that every woman who saw him wanted to be his, but he would have nothing to do with them. Even the most beautiful of the nymphs, Echo, could not move him. He scorned love with others because he loved only himself. He was punished by the goddess Nemesis, who made him fall in love with his reflection. We must look at his story metaphorically and see Narcissus as the self-loving person who has no love or concern for others and, thus involved with himself and his own well-being, ultimately destroys himself. In this respect he is a paradigmatic hero of consumer culture: so involved with himself and his purchases that he has no time or love to give to others.

There is, I must add, a dynamism to consumer cultures; the problem in most consumer cultures is that goods are distributed so unequally. Recent events in Russia and Eastern Europe have shown that people want a consumer culture—that is, they want goods and services that will make their lives easier and more pleasurable. The problem we face now is how to modify our consumer cultures so that there is more equality and justice. Has the institution of advertising so affected our psyches, so transformed and remolded our sensuality, that we cannot escape from our consumer lust and our narcissistic individualism?

The Politicization of Everyday Life

That is the question we face in our postmodern societies, and the resolution of that question will shape our everyday lives. Our everyday lives are to a great extent private (at least our mornings are, as I tried to suggest), but we cannot escape the realm of the political, which impinges, ultimately, on every aspect of our lives. As Claus Mueller explains in *The Politics of Communication*, the intervention of the state into realms such as education, the economy, and social services has had a direct impact on our lives and has led to the politicization of everyday life.

In the nineteenth century, he suggests, individuals were subjected to the authority of the state in relatively few areas. This has changed as the state has become, through its regulations and the growth of governmental institutions and bureaucracies, of central importance in our lives. As Mueller writes, "It is the dissolution of the borderline between the private and public realms that politicizes everyday life. Discontent over access to education and meaningful work, social discrimination, the quality of urban life, pollution of the environment, inflation, unemployment, taxation, transportation, medical costs—in short, the entire spectrum of the sectorial crisis—has found an easily defined locus since the state and 'politics' are held responsible" (1973, 161, 162).

We have a new sense now of the relationships between our everyday lives and the social order and see government as being responsible for what happens to us and to others. As the problem of classes and the unequal distribution of goods becomes more acute, there results a delegitimization of the authority of government, a process we see growing in contemporary American society.

Everyday life, then, is tied intimately to our political order, though it may seem that our everyday lives are our own affairs and that social and political considerations are far removed from, if not irrelevant to, our daily activities. It is here, then, that the extremes touch. What seemed to be a private realm, our own "dominion" in the privacy of our own houses, ends up, we see, intimately tied to the social and political order in which we find ourselves. Private decisions, we now recognize, have public consequences, and public decisions, it turns out, have an impact on our everyday lives—whether we are aware of it or not.

If we are like Narcissus, so involved with our own everyday lives, so "in love" with ourselves that we have no love for anyone else (including, often, even members of our own families) and no concern for their well-being, ironically, we end up destroying the fabric of society that sustains everyone and, thus, ultimately, ourselves. That is why Auden's line is so telling: "We must love one another or die."

References

Baker, Nicholson. 1988. *The Mezzanine.* New York: Weidenfeld & Nicolson.

Barthes, Roland. 1972. *Mythologies.* Translated by Annette Lavers. New York: Hill & Wang.

_____. 1982. *Empire of Signs.* Translated by Richard Howard. New York: Hill & Wang.

_____. 1988. *The Semiotic Challenge.* Translated by Richard Howard. New York: Hill & Wang.

Berger, Arthur Asa. 1970. *The Evangelical Hamburger: Essays on Commonplace Aspects of American Culture and Society.* New York: MSS Publications.

_____. 1989. *Signs in Contemporary Culture: An Introduction to Semiotics.* New York: Longman.

_____. 1992. *Reading Matter: Multidisciplinary Perspectives on Material Culture.* New Brunswick, N.J.: Transaction Publishers.

Berger, John. 1972. *Ways of Seeing.* New York: Penguin Books.

Braudel, Fernand. 1981. *The Structures of Everyday Life: The Limits of the Possible.* New York: Harper & Row.

Camus, Albert. 1966. *The Myth of Sisyphus and Other Essays.* Translated by Justin O'Brien. New York: Knopf.

Certeau, Michel de. 1984. *The Practice of Everyday Life.* Translated by Steven Rendall. Berkeley: University of California Press.

_____. 1986. *Heterologies: Discourses on the Other.* Translated by Brian Massumi. Minneapolis: University of Minnesota Press.

Dahlberg, Edward. 1960. *Can These Bones Live.* New York: New Directions.

Davis, Robert Con, and Ronald Schleifer. 1991. *Criticism and Culture.* New York: Longman.

Debord, Guy. 1970. *Society of the Spectacle.* Detroit: Black and Red.

Douglas, Jack D., Patricia A. Adler, Peter Adler, Andrea Fontana, C. Robert Freeman, and Joseph A. Kotarka. 1980. *Introduction to the Sociologies of Everyday Life.* Boston: Allyn & Bacon.

Douglas, Mary. 1966. *Purity and Danger: An Analysis of the Concepts of Pollution and Taboo.* New York: Praeger.

_____. 1975. *Implicit Meanings.* London: Routledge & Kegan Paul.

Dye, Thomas, and L. Harmon Ziegler. 1975. *The Irony of Democracy.* North Scituate, Mass.: Duxbury Press.

Eliade, Mircea. 1958. *Patterns of Comparative Religion.* New York: Sheed & Ward.

_____. 1961. *The Sacred and the Profane.* New York: Harper Torchbooks.

Featherstone, Mike. 1991. *Consumer Culture and Postmodernism.* Thousand Oaks, Calif.: Sage Publications.

Forty, Adrian. 1986. *Objects of Desire: Design and Society from Wedgwood to IBM.* New York: Pantheon Books.

Freud, Sigmund. 1963. *Character and Culture.* Edited by Phillip Rieff. New York: Collier Books.

_____. 1965. *The Interpretation of Dreams.* New York: Avon Books.

Fromm, Erich. 1971. *Beyond the Chains of Illusion: My Encounter with Marx and Freud.* New York: Simon and Schuster.

Giedion, Siegfried. 1969. *Mechanization Takes Command.* New York: W. W. Norton.

Hamilton, Edith. 1953. *Mythology.* New York: Mentor Books.

Haug, Wolfgang Fritz. 1986. *Critique of Commodity Aesthetics: Appearance, Sexuality and Advertising in Capitalist Society.* Minneapolis: University of Minnesota Press.

Huizinga, Johan. 1924. *The Waning of the Middle Ages.* Garden City, N.Y.: Doubleday Anchor Books.

Ionesco, Eugene. 1958. *Four Plays.* New York: Grove Press.

Joyce, James. 1934. *Ulysses.* New York: Random House.

Lefebvre, Henri. 1971. *Everyday Life in the Modern World.* New York: Harper Torchbooks.

References

Lodge, David, ed. 1988. *Modern Criticism and Theory.* New York: Longman.

McLuhan, Marshall. 1967. *The Mechanical Bride: Folklore of Industrial Man.* Boston: Beacon Press.

Mueller, Claus. 1975. *The Politics of Communication.* New York: Oxford University Press.

Murray, Henry A., ed. 1968. *Myth and Mythmaking.* Boston: Beacon Press.

Rank, Otto. 1964. *The Myth of the Birth of the Hero.* New York: Vintage Books.

Rossi, William A. 1976. *The Sex Life of the Foot and Shoe.* New York: Saturday Review Press and E. P. Dutton.

Saussure, Ferdinand de. 1966. *Course in General Linguistics.* New York: McGraw-Hill.

Thompson, Michael. 1979. *Rubbish Theory: The Creation and Destruction of Value.* Oxford: Oxford University Press.

About the Book
and Author

King-sized beds, comforters, gel toothpaste, razors, underwear, the morning shower—all activities and objects we have tended to pay no attention to—until the publication of this book. In a series of short vignettes endearingly illustrated by the author, Arthur Asa Berger gives Americans a profound way to understand their morning rituals.

Have you ever considered, for instance, that the digital clock, by producing free-floating liquid numerals disconnecting us from both time past and time future, could be interpreted as a metaphor for the alienation many people feel in contemporary society? Or consider our nightclothes: The pajama is the most immediate witness to our sexual activities; thus, we cover our pajamas with a bathrobe to guard against the anxiety of being revealed to other family members. The pajama is intricately connected to human shame.

Bloom's Morning, with thirty-six short chapters bracketed by brief theoretical essays on the nature of semiotic analysis, is a perfect book for the inquisitive mind. It is chock-full of valuable and quirky nuggets from this most interesting of social commentators—items that, taken together, give us a new vision through which to understand ourselves.

Arthur Asa Berger is professor of broadcast and electronic communication arts at San Francisco State University, where he has taught since 1965. He has published more than thirty books on popular culture, media, and everyday life.

Index

Index